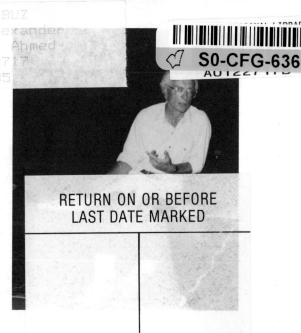

RETURN ON OR BEFORE
LAST DATE MARKED

ALEX BUZO .... and educated at The
Armidale Schoo................................ South Wales. In the
1960s he was .... style of Australian
playwriting wit................................ *Ahmed, Rooted, The*
Front Room Bo............................

In 1972-3 .... with the Melbourne
Theatre Compan............................. were premiered. Then
followed *Coral* ....), *Martello Towers*
(1976), *Makass*.......................... 980), *The Marginal*
Farm (1983), *S*........................ *Road* (1989), which
have been perfo........................... Nimrod in Sydney
to the Arena Sta........................... made into a telemovie
by ABC-TV, wh................................ *Lansdowne Says No*, and
in 1988 Film Australia released its version of *Norm and Ahmed.*

Norm and Ahmed is one of the most widely performed
Australian plays with revivals in Sydney in 1981 (directed by the
author), London in 1983, Melbourne 1987, Kuala Lumpur 1989, Los
Angeles 1990, Adelaide 1991 and Sydney at the Griffin Theatre
1991 where it was followed by a revival of *Rooted.*

As well as writing plays and working in radio, television and
film, Alex Buzo has written a number of books: *Tautology, Meet the*
New Class, The Search for Harry Allway, Glancing Blows, The
Young Person's Guide to the Theatre, The Longest Game and *Prue*
Flies North. He has also contributed chapters to *Country*
Childhoods, The Great Literacy Debate and *Writers In Action.*

Bruce Wedderburn as Bentley and Gilda Proietti as Sandy in the Just Kidding production of *Rooted* at the Stables Theatre, 9 May 1991. Photographer: Allen Fox.

NORM & AHMED
AND
Other Plays

ALEX BUZO

Macquarie
Regional Library

CURRENCY PRESS • SYDNEY

CURRENCY PLAYS
General Editor: Katharine Brisbane

First published in 1973 by
Currency Methuen Drama Pty Ltd.
Norm and Ahmed first published in 1969
in *Komos*, Vol. 2 No 2.
Reprinted in 1977, 1979, 1993
by Currency Press Pty Ltd
PO Box 452, Paddington
NSW 2021, Australia

National Library of Australia
Cataloguing-in-Publication data
　　Buzo, Alexander, 1944-
　　　　[Norm and Ahmed; Rooted; The Roy Murphy Show]. Norm and
　　　　Ahmed and other plays.

　　ISBN 0 86819007 1

　　　　I. Title. II. Title: Rooted. III. Title: Roy Murphy Show. IV. Title:
　　　　Norm and Ahmed; Rooted; The Roy Murphy Show.

　A822.3

Cover photo shows Max Cullen as Norm and Alex Pinder as Ahmed. Cover
photo by Roslyn Sharp. Reproduced by kind permission of Film Australia.
Printed by Southwood Press, Marrickville, NSW.

CONTENTS

	page
Introduction	vii
NORM AND AHMED	1
ROOTED	27
THE ROY MURPHY SHOW	101
Notes and Glossary	135

To Merelyn

POINTS OF REFERENCE

'You've got to have a point of reference', says Bentley in
Rooted. Points of reference are basic to Alexander
Buzo's approach to the business of playwriting. Still only
28, he has been as long as he can remember a surprised
voyeur of Australian mores. Later, what began as a
curiosity became a professional skill which he uses with
the patience and relentlessness of the birdwatcher.

A native-born Australian brought up in a country
town, he has a background more accurately described
as part-international than part-immigrant; and which
has been to some degree responsible for the detachment
of his writing.

Among contemporary playwrights he is in a minority
in having grown up in middle-class security; and while
he involves himself as closely as any of them in the
problems of Australian urban society and the study of
the Australian character, Buzo is alone in viewing them
not from the centre of the imbroglio but from his chosen
observation post. Paradoxically, his plays in performance
are notable for a close identification by the audience
with the principal characters; but the author's attitude
remains ambivalent.

He is unique among those writers at present working
in the Australian theatre in being a stylist in the first
instance. His chosen tools are those of exactitude, not of
passion; and he makes himself understood initially
through his style rather than his material. Buzo has been
recognised as deeply a Sydney writer: the apparently
superficial dazzle of his work is very much a Sydney
method; and the medley of brassy hedonism and
deprived sensitivity as he is able to express it, has its
roots in Sydney society. Though his characters are
recognised and acknowledged by the rest of Australia

and have found their equivalent social groups abroad, in Sydney they can be traced to their very suburb and place of work. In no other contemporary Australian playwright is the writing so clinically local as in Buzo.

The first aspect of his writing to strike his audience is his acute reproduction of the Australian vernacular. He is a frequenter of public bars, of committee rooms, of public meetings and sports meetings, anywhere where a homogeneous group of Australians meet and exchange their particular and distinct lingo. In his play **The Front Room Boys** (1969) he exposes the public service style of jargon; in **The Roy Murphy Show** (1971) the incongruously pedantic language of the sports commentator; in **Tom** (1972) a mixed vocabulary of advertising and big business; in **Rooted** (1969) we have a variety of styles, from Bentley's public service language to that of surfies, art gallery jargon, and the social cliché which is designed specifically to mean nothing at all.

It is not, however, verisimilitude he is after. The basis of his comic style is the juxtaposition of words and phrases which by their incongruity ensure that they make their impact.

He is not a naturalistic writer. His phrases are not there as indications of the inner life of the characters, like the top of an iceberg. The phrases are their life, both inner and outer. Nothing is left unsaid or undone – except perhaps in the case of **Macquarie** (1971) in which he abandons his love of the vernacular phrase to examine the origins of that sense of you-can't-buck-the-system hopelessness which pursues the characters in his other plays.

Buzo has often referred to an early devotion to comic books and sees some influence upon his writing. A comparison with the two-dimensional comic book style in which the odds against the hero are of cosmic proportions and the characters say exactly what they think, reserving nothing, is of some value. But while the characters may be at times startlingly simple the situations in which they find themselves make ripples through our own experience which grow wider as we watch.

The most orthodox naturalistic play by Alexander

Buzo is his first successful piece, **Norm and Ahmed** (1968), which remains today a minor classic. It contains an old theme and a new one, both of which are crucial to the understanding of present-day Australia.

The old theme is the sense of alienation which has been with the Australian ever since the first fleet of British were exiled against their will from their homeland to the other side of the world. In two hundred years the Australian has never really come to terms with his land, though he would defend it with his last breath as God's own country. Norm Gallagher is a typical example of a certain kind of puzzled middle-aged Australian who has felt this alienation and yet never understood it.

The new theme this small play offers is a place for Australia in an Asian context – something that until this time has not been done in the theatre except in reference to the war in the Pacific. **Norm and Ahmed** is a midnight conversation between a Pakistani student and a cliché-familiar Australian workman; and what emerges not only confronts us with how little Norm and his fellow Australians understand about Asians but with how close Australia is to its near north. Both Norm and Ahmed, says Buzo perceptively, are aliens in the same country.

Buzo has written nothing better of its kind than his portrait of Norm Gallagher, the 'average Australian', a collection of urban clichés from popular literature. Norm is the typical RSL man, the supporter of law and order and laissez-faire, the sportsman, the club man, a faithful cog in the wheel of industry, an almost white-collar worker. And looked at more closely, he is much more. Take the opening sequence of **Norm and Ahmed.** Norm is idling on a city footpath at midnight, waiting to strike up a conversation with someone. The situation is suspicious to say the least. All Norm wants is a conversation – desperately, appearances indicate – but the aggressive defensiveness which is so much part of the Australian character leaps at us immediately.

> NORM: What's the matter, mate? Do you think I'm going to hold you up and rob you or something?
>
> AHMED: *(hastily)* Oh, no, not at all.
>
> NORM: This isn't India, mate. You're in Sydney. No Bombay stranglers around here. You're quite safe.

Here we have it. The point of reference. God's own country.

Norm is proud of his country but he does not attempt to understand it. For him it is a hole he can run to. Listen to him trying to explain the White Australia Policy. Or the unionist activities of his father. Or anything, in fact, that is outside his immediate experience. Confronted with a direct threat to himself he reacts swiftly and violently; confronted with the unfamiliar he is immediately out of his depth. His language becomes comically pretentious and his response each time is to defend authority, wherever it is. 'You can't buck the system,' he says. Take the contradiction in his view about the police. Here is the double-think that makes Buzo's chess characters both comic and pitiful.

AHMED: Sometimes I feel the police deserve some form of retaliation from their victims.

NORM: Ar, come on Ahmed, give the coppers a fair go. They're not such bad blokes. Give them a break. They're just doing their job, that's all. They only want to preserve law and order in the community. Mind you, though, if a mug copper ever started pushing me around, I'd job him good and proper, no risk about that. I don't take no crap from no one. But, by the same token, Ahmed, I reckon our policemen are doing a pretty good job and I'd do all that's in my power, all that's humanly possible to assist them in the performance of their duties. Go easy on the old wallopers, that's what I say, give the coppers a fair go.

A fair go. A fair day's work for a fair day's pay. The answers to all the problems.

Tiny as they are Norm does have his roots which hold him steady in the face of the alien world. The first is prejudice which enables him to hold opinions with courage and firmness, if not clarity. The second is his house and family. The echoes of Barry Humphries' Sandy Stone are strong as he talks about his home, his dear wife Beryl, who 'played a good game of bowls in her twilight years'; and 'the time we danced all night at the Bronte R.S.L'. He suffers the same uncomprehending loneliness as Sandy Stone, and takes the same joy in his suburban amusements; and the same stunted but genuine aesthetic pleasure in his growing garden.

Why in the end does Norm kick Ahmed when each of them has made some confidences, has expressed some mutual respect and parted with protestations of goodwill? Because in his own mind some judgment is required of him and no authority is at hand to guide him. It is not like the occasion at Tobruk when he caught a German prisoner and, after beating him nearly to death 'handed him over to the proper authorities'. Nor like the trade unionists at his mother's house whom the police took away, nor the mug copper whom he won't let push him around. From Ahmed he has received only politeness and an inexplicable reserve in which he smells superiority. And that is the only thing the free white Australian cannot stand. His powers of reasoning may have betrayed him in the past but his prejudice he can rely upon. 'Fuckin' boongs', he says.

Bentley in **Rooted** could very well be Norm's son Bernie, who is studying 'well . . . technology, you know' at the Massachusetts Institute of Technology. Bentley is another generation removed from the old prejudices and has no roots at all. This is the core of Bentley's tragedy.

When the play opens Bentley is surrounded by his tangible proofs of being 'on the way up' – his tight little home unit and tight little wife; and his expensive products of technology – his stereo and his tape recorders.

But from then on his castle begins to crumble.

In the battle between man and machine the machine always wins. Technology leaves no margin for error. Bentley's opponent, the invisible Simmo, is a concatenation of this world in which men become machines. He is the master-mind at the apex of the well-oiled business machine: the embodiment of all those men one has envied – dux of the school, star of the football team, Casanova, war hero, self-made man, superman, chairman of directors. The man always two steps ahead of one's own road to success.

Simmo wins hands down because his mystery is success. He never appears because for this he would have to be burdened with some human caparison – and by implication some human weakness, at least in the audience's mind – and Simmo's one quality is that his armour of righteousness is invincible. Buzo has chosen a style with cumulative situations and stereotype characters which come very close to comic strip frames. Each scene tends to deal with a single aspect of the total awfulness of Bentley's situation, as if he is being walled up brick by brick like the Canterville Ghost. But though the style is farcical the problem with which Bentley is confronted is wholly serious in its implications.

It is the same problem which has made Norm what he is, which has made him run to earth among his frangipani, fearful to form any opinion of the society in which he lives, falling back instead upon an ill-founded faith in the idols of authority that society has made for itself. Poor Bentley has no sanctuary. Not even his home is inviolate. In the opening scene he is at a peak of satisfaction ('everyone raved about the unit') which he never reaches again. Firstly Sandy: there's 'this thing with Simmo'. He is torn between the feelings of an outraged husband and an unwillingness to speak out of turn against a natural superior.

Take the first mention of Simmo in scene 1:

> What was it? Well, I'll tell you, darling. You see, I noticed Simmo paying you a lot of attention tonight. He left the keg twice to talk to you. So I sort of took him aside and said, 'Look, Simmo, I know you're a big mover with the birds, but Sandy's my wife, so I'd just like to sort of . . . ascertain your intentions . . . as it were'.
>
> *(Pause.)*
>
> He told me to get stuffed.
>
> *(Pause.)*
>
> Huh. Funny bloke, Simmo. You want to watch out for him. Still, I know there's nothing in it.
>
> *(Pause.)*
>
> I wouldn't get . . . involved with Simmo, if I were you.
>
> *(Pause.)*
>
> Still, I know there's nothing in it.

Bentley's whole predicament is there committed to paper. He is transparent: the little man defending his castle with ludicrously inadequate weapons. See how the words shift under his feet. Once or twice he is on solid ground with matters he understands: 'He left the keg twice to talk to you' and 'He told me to get stuffed'.

But the whole sequence has that dying fall which tells you in the rhythm that Bentley hasn't a chance. And this rhythm is repeated again and again in such small clauses as the speech to Simmo quoted, which opens so bravely and ends so lamely, and in the shape of the whole play.

It is not insignificant that it is only in the last few seconds of the play, when Bentley has run his course and has nothing more to lose, that the barriers between him and the other characters fall, the clichés vanish and some moment of rapport is reached. Bentley, of course, is silent.

The environment of **Rooted** is also carefully evoked to point up the conflicting yearnings inside the young middle-class men like Bentley. His yearning after natural freedom as described in his morning walk on the beach contrasts savagely with the technological marvel of his home unit. The sun and sand of the surfie world hovers about the play and enters it in the second act in the persons of Gary and Diane. But the attempts to introduce qualitative elements into the lives of the group, as exemplified by Richard's dabble at literature and painting, are pathetically inadequate and demonstrate as in the other aspects of the play the gap between private day-dreams and the energy and comprehension required for achievement. Sensation, finally, is the nearest they get to sensitivity – the surfari, the country weekend, the joy ride in the beach buggy. The people, the experiences, the women out of their reach they denigrate. Those within their grasp they discard with a uniform disappointment which comes from their own stunted ability to respond to life. Each of the characters has individual ambitions; and we last see them – except Bentley whose crime is that he does not 'fit in' – in the uniform business suit of Simmo Enterprises. This is the road to the things that really matter, says Buzo ironically. Right through the background of the play is the gentle deflation of the myth of the bronzed Sydney hedonist.

There are two consistent dramatic tools in the play which are important to the fall of Bentley. The first is silence, the second is light. Silence is the one effective weapon in **Rooted**. Sandy uses it repeatedly against Bentley. She does not argue, she demolishes him by

refusing to recognise him as a combatant. Silence in the
play is seldom companionable. The pauses are aggressive, they speak as loudly as the words. Sandy's silence
with Bentley is all the more belligerent because when she
really meets a worthy opponent like the dry-cleaning
firm, she can talk like a machine gun.

The ultimate in silence is, of course, Simmo, the
power in the other room, always just out of sight, who
cannot be subdued with words. Only Bentley is unable
to use his silence effectively – until the last page of the
text. His silences are variations of awkwardness, invita-
tions to responses that never come; and much of his talk
is a desperate alternative to silence. The pauses lose their
energy as Bentley's strength flags. Only at the end when
all the masks have dropped away does silence give him
some dignity. It envelopes him, like the enclosing
darkness and makes the birthday celebration by contrast
garish. Having lost all, being 'rooted' in the slang sense
of the title, Bentley does finally find his point of reference.

As a dramatic device Simmo is not entirely a success.
I have not seen the play work really successfully in
regard to Simmo, though within the play's structure he
fits quite logically. The extended expectation is an idea
easier to sustain in a novel than in the theatre, especially
when one's programme confirms that Simmo is not going
to materialise to climax the third act. But Bentley is a
man with whom every audience can only too easily
identify. He is a confirmation of all our worst fears.

The light imagery too follows the rhythm of the play.

The stage directions are quite specific. Bentley's home
unit is all white, except for two blue armchairs. It is a
light, tight, bright room in which Bentley lives. The first
intrusion that mars the room is Sandy's black dress on
the ironing board. In scene three Bentley, in whites,
gives us his first insight into his private dreams:

> It was sunny now, people around, splashing in the sand.
> There was sunlight splattered all over the place. All over
> the sea, all over the sand, all over me. Sunlight everywhere.
> Sparkling. Then I came back here. You were still asleep.
> I looked at you. Like a baby.
>
> (Pause.)
>
> It was a beautiful walk.

This is Bentley's view of paradise, the familiar Australian joy in the sun and the sea. Within a few minutes Sandy is telling him he is a ghost, the light has gone out of the marriage and he must leave the unit. From then on poor Bentley is a hollow man, going through the rituals of living, playing host to a schoolfriend he cannot remember, talking over the old barroom conventions and adolescent sex games. He and the audience lose the power to distinguish between real and imaginary recollections but he clings on just the same. The more he seeks to make them tangible, as his tape recorder had been tangible, the more they elude him. Between him and the others there is an invisible curtain and others are acting out their dreams too – Sandy, describing her panty-hose commercial, Richard playing the artist, Diane playing first one kind of girl friend and then another. None of these people are what they say they are. They parrot the language and the ritual gestures, as if that is enough to transform them.

The arrival of Simmo in the unit at the beginning of Act Two is marked by his red abstract painting. Sandy hangs it up and its colour in the immaculate, sterile room is obscene. It is 6 p.m. now. The evening is closing in. Sandy goes out into the night. In the next scene it is still dusk and Sandy is preparing a candlelight supper. But in scene three it is 10 o'clock on the following night, and Bentley is expelled from the bedroom. By the end of the act Bentley has been turned out, disconsolately and with a massive fantasy effort at dignity, into the darkness.

Act Three opens to reveal a black curtain, before which dangles a meat pie.

Behind the curtain is the room he is to live in. The walls are brown and it has more than one bad painting intruding into it. It has dozens. He takes over a dirty room and a second-hand life.

Bentley makes one last shuddering attempt to recall his pristine hedonism. In the middle of a medley of recollections which neither he nor Richard can quite distinguish he describes a walk he had taken in a nearby park. But this time it is cool and windy and he tries to recall his childhood by swinging on a willow tree by a pond. There is no joy to be found. He falls in.

From then on the end is swift. Simmo pursues him even to his last penurious hideout and the end is inevitable and black.

He goes without a struggle because he has been deprived of Norm's summary form of self-defence – physical assault – without providing himself with another. Bentley is incapable of Norm's prejudices because he is a processed white-collar worker with a secondary education which has succeeded in substituting words for fists without teaching how words can be used effectively.

The Roy Murphy Show, which brings Buzo into the field of pure satire, is a literal interpretation of the problem of the 'rooted' man. Roy Murphy's Simmo really is a machine – the television – and through it he receives the life force which motivates him. Basically, the play is about one's capacity, or lack of it, to control one's life.

At the opening of the play Roy is, on the whole, managing very well. He is sitting at his controller's desk with three telephones. Through these he is connected by electronic tentacles to Sir Roland Dalrymple, the owner of the TV station and also his father-in-law, to the wife who has threatened to divorce him and to the mistress who is waiting for him. And when the light goes on he is plugged into the millions of viewers who watch The World of Sportsview Roundup Highlights.

Roy in his way is master of a little empire and by the judicious use of the machine, he keeps it under control. We admire his multi-lingual dexterity – one language for Sir Roland, another for the viewers, a third for the technicians. We find he has a lisp which he has learnt to control. But gradually his world, like Bentley's, begins to disintegrate. Just as order in the kingdom in the Elizabethan world stemmed from the king, so when the cracks begin to appear in the character of Roy Murphy the world about him begins to crumble. He is not an obvious victim, as Bentley is, but he does turn out to be a mechanical man, stuffed full of recordings of second-hand words. When the recordings run down and the light goes off then it is as if Roy Murphy had never existed.

Murphy's use of words is like his use of machinery, to keep himself intact and other people at arm's length.

His sentences do not fade away into three dots as Bentley's do. Murphy uses words as Norm uses his fists, against all comers.

The fight is not one of finesse but it is effective until the realities at the other end of the phone begin to penetrate and sap his concentration. As his fingers relax on the controls, tempers begin to flare and the real personalities of his companions are displayed naked to their shocked audience.

The TV man's nightmare into which the show deteriorates is not only a satire of the medium and those who run it. It embodies the worst fears of that verbose majority which Norm represents and which places its faith in authority for no better reason than that authority exists. The fears are that any weakening of the bulwarks against individual choice, any loosening of the rules of behaviour, will open the floodgates to a wave of moral pollution such as we see in **The Roy Murphy Show.** Buzo's answer to the disaster is, of course, a facetious one – the oldest of Australian jokes: when control and command are needed for a local problem, call in an overseas expert.

The Roy Murphy Show is a slighter piece than the other two but it confirms Norm's unsteady values and his conviction that the system always wins, however absurd it is. The aspect of both **Norm and Ahmed** and **Rooted** that in this play he takes to its furthest extremity is the defensive use of the vernacular which becomes at its purest a code of behaviour of considerable subtlety.

So much of the language which Buzo records so accurately is rooted in the paradoxical impulse which leads Norm to kick Ahmed. It rises from a deep defensive aggression which in turn rises from a deep inability to make steady moral decisions. The rules of the game played in these pieces call for friendly gestures, a spurious open-faced matiness which derives from the manners of the old bush days when every new face was a welcome one. But what, in Buzo's observation, the outback friendliness hides is an urban terror of proximity, involvement and responsibility – a way of using words to not listen, not learn and not understand.

Katharine Brisbane   *March* 1973

Edwin Hodgeman as Ahmed and Ron Graham as Norm in the Old Tote Theatre production of *Norm and Ahmed*, Sydney 1968, directed by Jim Sharman. Photo: Robert Walker.

Norm and Ahmed

CHARACTERS

NORM, *a strongly-built, middle-aged man.*

AHMED, *a slim young Pakistani student.*

SCENE

A footpath on a Sydney street under some scaffolding in front of a construction site. A white fence at the back, about five feet high, and then a wire-mesh fence rising above it. The scaffolding is supported by two posts at the front, which are joined by a handrail. There is a bus stop on one side and a garbage tin on the other.

TIME

Midnight on a summer night.

Norm and Ahmed was first performed by the Old Tote Theatre Company at the Old Tote Theatre, Sydney, on April 9th, 1968, with the following cast:

NORM	Ron Graham
AHMED	Edwin Hodgeman

Setting designed by Allan Lees

Directed by Jim Sharman

Lights up on NORM, *who is leaning against the fence. He wears an open necked white shirt and grey trousers. A clock strikes twelve.* NORM *moves around restlessly looking up and down the street. He takes out a cigarette packet, looks in it, then screws it up and flings it on the ground angrily. He brings out a fresh packet, rips off the cellophane with his teeth and takes out a cigarette, which he lights with a lighter. He moves around a bit more and then leans on the fence again. He waits. Then he starts moving around some more, and suddenly straightens up, looking to his left. He puts his cigarette out and takes another from the packet, putting it in his mouth unlit. He leans casually against the fence. The sound of footsteps is heard and* AHMED *appears, wearing a Nehru-style suit and carrying a briefcase. He walks past* NORM.

NORM: Excuse me, mate.
(AHMED *stops and looks at* NORM. *Pause.*)
   Got a light?
AHMED: Yes, certainly.
(He offers a box of matches.)
NORM: Thanks.
(He keeps the matches after he has lit up.)
   I was dying for a smoke. Lucky you turned up. Nothing open at this hour.
AHMED: No, it's nearly midnight.
(Pause. AHMED *has been waiting for* NORM *to return his matches, but now he starts to edge away warily.)*
NORM: Wait a minute, mate.
AHMED: Yes?
(Pause.)
NORM: You forgot your matches.
(He holds them out.)
AHMED: *(taking them warily)* Thank you.
(He edges away.)
NORM: What's the matter, mate? Do you think I'm going to hold you up and rob you or something?
AHMED: *(hastily)* Oh no, not at all.
NORM: This isn't India, mate. You're in Sydney. No Bombay stranglers around here. You're quite safe.

3

AHMED: There are hoodlums here, too. Just as many as in my country.

NORM: Yeah, I'd reckon it'd be about evens. What part of the . . . uh . . . south-east Asian sub-continent would you be from?

AHMED: I am from Pakistan. Karachi, to be exact. I, uh, really must be going . . .

NORM: Eh, wait a minute, mate. I'm not going to rob you or bash you or anything.

AHMED: I was not suggesting for one minute that you were.

NORM: Then what's the matter, you think I'm a drunk? You think I'm one of those old piss-pots who go around the place annoying decent people?

AHMED: No, not at all.

NORM: You think I'm a poofter, then, don't you? That's what you're thinking, isn't it? You think I'm like those poofters in Hyde Park who go around soliciting blokes.

AHMED: Certainly not. I assure you I think nothing of the kind. I hope I have not insulted you in any way. If I have, I crave your forgiveness.

NORM: Ar, she's right. I suppose you've got to be careful these days. Lot of nasty types around.

AHMED: Yes, there is a lot of violence prevalent at the moment.

NORM: Too right. You look a bit uneasy.

AHMED: I do?

NORM: Yes. Are you sure you're all right?

AHMED: Yes.

NORM: You don't look all right.

AHMED: I feel fine.

NORM: My name's Norm Gallagher, what's yours?

AHMED: My name is Ahmed. *(Moving away)* Well, I don't wish to seem rude . . .

NORM: Pleased to meet you, Ahmed.

(He offers his hand.)

AHMED: *(shaking hands)* How do you do?

NORM: Pakistan. Now that's an interesting place. I've never been to Pakistan. I was in Egypt during the war, but we never went anywhere else. How do you like Australia?

AHMED: It is a very nice place. Naturally I tend to get a little home-sick at times, but I quite like it out here. The people are very friendly.

NORM: It's good to hear that, Ahmed. You feel you're settling down all right?

AHMED: Yes, I think so. One always experiences difficulties when one is seeking to adjust to an alien environment. But once the initial period of adjustment is over, it is easier to acclimatise oneself.

(Pause.)

NORM: That's very true.

AHMED: Yes. Now if you'll excuse me, I'll . . .

NORM: Do you know what? You're insulting me, do you know that? Eh? You're insinuating that I'm some kind of drunken pervert.

AHMED: Oh no, you have misconstrued my actions. I think nothing of the kind.

NORM: Then why do you keep backing away, eh? Answer me that.

AHMED: Well . . . I mean . . . it's late. It's late at night.

NORM: I know it's late. That's no reason. You think you're a bit above me. You don't want to talk to me. I'm insulted. If you think I'm a drunken perv, why don't you say so? Why don't you come right out and say it?

AHMED: I'm very sorry if you think that. Perhaps I have shown bad manners. I offer my humble apologies.

NORM: Never been so insulted in all . . .

AHMED: Please! Believe me. I did not mean to be rude.

NORM: You sure?

AHMED: Of course I'm sure.

NORM: Well, all right then, don't worry about it. Just a bit of a misunderstanding, that's all. No hard feelings. Jees, I tell you what, Ahmed, you really looked scared there for a minute.

(He laughs.)

AHMED: *(smiling, relieved)* Did I really?

NORM: *(jovially)* Yeah, you were terrified. You looked as if a kick in the crutch and a cold frankfurt'd finish you off. You're all right now?

AHMED: Yes.

NORM: ⎫You sure?

AHMED:⎭Yes.

NORM: No worries?

AHMED: No.

NORM: You sure?

AHMED: Yes.

NORM: Everything's fine?

AHMED: Yes.

(Pause.)

NORM: You sure?

AHMED: Yes! Yes! I am sure!

NORM: *(prowling around Ahmed)* Good. I'm pleased to hear that. That's very encouraging. Where do you live, Ahmed?

AHMED: I am at La Perouse, not far from the university. I'm sharing a flat with some Indian students.

NORM: La Perouse, eh? What, right out at Botany Bay?

AHMED: Yes. The flat overlooks the bay.

NORM: That's where it all started, isn't it? That's where old Captain Cook landed, Botany Bay. Must have given the boongs a fright, eh? I mean, the aborigines were probably quite surprised to see the white men in their big ships. All those sails in the wind. They probably thought the white man was some kind of monster.

AHMED: That's quite possible.

NORM: You know much about Australian history?

AHMED: No, not a great deal. I am studying it at the university.

NORM: You're out at the old brain drainer, eh? What course would you be taking, Ahmed?

AHMED: Arts. I am studying for a Bachelor of Arts degree.

NORM: Arts, eh? What, bit of a painter, are you?

AHMED: No, I am not doing painting, I am studying the humanities.

NORM: Oh. Uh . . . now just what exactly would that involve, Ahmed?

AHMED: History, mainly. I am majoring in History.

NORM: Oh, *History*. Yeah, I see. I was never much good at History. No head for dates. That was my trouble. Tell me, Ahmed, what with your education and all, you'd be able to form a few impressions, like, of this country. I mean, you'd be able to sort a few things out. Have your own opinions.

AHMED: Yes, I have formed several opinions of your country . . . some good, others bad.

NORM: What would you say was a bad point, Ahmed?

AHMED: Well, I would rather talk about the good points. It would hardly be diplomatic on my part to seek to undermine . . .

NORM: Ar come on, Ahmed, don't give us that. Don't be a creamer all your life. Tell me a bad point. The White Australia Policy, the way we govern ourselves, anything you like. I want you to tell me, right here and now, what you feel, in your own mind, is a bad thing in this country.

AHMED: Well then, if you are so keen to hear my opinion, I would say that . . . uh . . . well, for one thing, one of the, uh, less desirable aspects of your society, to my mind, would be the tendency of the mass media to be merely the mouthpiece of the big commercial and military interests . . . the, uh, free press, as it were. They brainwash the people. They . . . oh, please forgive me, I forget myself. As I said, it is not perhaps my place to seek to condemn your country. I have my own opinion, but I do not go around broadcasting it as it would not be the diplomatic thing to do.

NORM: Well, that's fair enough, Ahmed. I can see your point of view. For instance, if I went over to Pakistan, I wouldn't tell you blokes how to run your country.

I'd keep it to meself. I wouldn't throw me weight around in someone else's country. Mind you, I'd have me own opinion, though.

AHMED: Ah, that is quite right. I think you have put it most appositely, Norm. I have my own views but I observe a diplomatic silence.

NORM: That's a very sensible idea. I understand exactly how you must feel, Ahmed. When I was in Egypt during the war, I didn't think the Egyptians ran their country extra well. But I kept quiet, I didn't want to crool meself. And just between you and me and the garbage can, I didn't cotton much to the Egyptians themselves. We had our differences, I can tell you. I never took to them.

AHMED: A difficult race to understand, perhaps. I can readily appreciate the frustrations you must have experienced.

NORM: It's nice of you to say that, Ahmed, because these blokes *were* hard to understand. There were faults on both sides, of course, and there's two sides to every question, as you well know, but, well, there it is. I just didn't take to them. Might have been my fault. You see, they're a cunning lot, those Gyppos. Take you down as soon as look at you. Some of our blokes were easy pickings for those bastards. Fruit on the sideboard. That's what they were.

AHMED: How long were you over there?

NORM: Quite a while. During the desert campaign. I was in Tobruk, mate. I was one of the rats of Tobruk.

AHMED: That was quite a battle, wasn't it?

NORM: Yes, it was a pretty good scrap – but we held out, mate, we stuck to our guns. We fought with everything we had – I even knocked one of 'em down with me bare hands. It's true. He was a prisoner, trying to escape, but I apprehended him and jobbed him one. I can still remember that night – I was out for a stroll on the gravel, savouring my last cigarette, when I heard this click in the moonlight, see. So I hid in the shadows and had a screw at the compound. *(Miming)* Then I saw him. It was a Kraut, cutting through the wires, trying to escape from us, the A.I.F. So I jumped out and confronted him . . . I offered to take him quietly, but the bastard come at me with a knife. I just stood there, cool as the proverbial cucumber. Then we started circling each other in the dark, round and round and round. *(Circling* AHMED*)* Then all of a sudden I grabbed him *(grabs* AHMED *by the throat)* and I *(he suddenly releases the struggling* AHMED, *who breaks away and retreats a few paces, watching* NORM *warily)*. Jees, what have I done? Sorry, Ahmed, old mate. I got a bit carried away there for a minute. Are you all right?

AHMED: *(straightening his collar)* Uh . . . yes, I'm all right.

NORM: I just got too excited, Ahmed, and that's a fact. I hope you'll forgive me.

AHMED: *(not quite won over)* Oh, certainly.

NORM: You know how it is, you do your block, you don't know where you are. Sure you're all right?

AHMED: Quite sure.

NORM: What a thing to do! And you a visitor to this country. I don't know what you must think.

AHMED: Oh, don't worry about it, Norm. You got a little excited, that's all.

NORM: You'll probably go back to your country and tell 'em we're all a mob of savages out here.

AHMED: *(profusely)* Not at all, Norm, not at all. I will do nothing of the kind.

NORM: You'll go back there and spread the word that we're all barbarians out here.

AHMED: No, no, I will do no such thing.

NORM: Don't know what came over me.

AHMED: Believe me, Norm, it's all right. No harm has been done.

NORM: You'll forgive me then?

AHMED: Of course, of course.

(Norm looks at him, smiles and pats him on the back.)

NORM: Good on you, Ahmed, old mate. You're a good
   sport. Here, have a cigarette.

(He offers a packet.)

AHMED: Thank you.

*(AHMED takes a cigarette and puts it in his mouth. He
fumbles in his pocket for matches. NORM brings out his
cigarette lighter and flicks it on. AHMED leans over to light
his cigarette, but stops a few inches short of the lighter. He looks
at the burning flame and then takes the cigarette out of his mouth
and looks at NORM, who is beaming benignly at him. He
looks at the flame again, hesitates, then finally puts the cigarette
in his mouth and lights it from the flame.)*

NORM: Anyway, Ahmed, as I was telling you, I floored
   this bloody Kraut. Really laid him out. He was all
   over the place like a mad woman's lunch box. Just
   lying there waiting for me to kill him. But do you
   know what I did?

AHMED: No, Norm, I have no idea.

NORM: I spared him. That's what I did. I could never
   kill a man in cold blood, Ahmed. It's not in my code
   of ethics. Not what I call doing the right thing. Human
   life is sacred, Ahmed, that's my firm belief. So I took
   him back to the compound and handed him over to
   the proper authorities without laying a hand on him.
   I was the hero of the whole battalion after that little
   effort, I can tell you. I was the toast of Tobruk, and
   that's the gospel truth. You do believe me, don't you?

AHMED: Why, of course, Norm.

NORM: It's as true as I'm standing here. And if I tell a
   lie, then may the Good Lord strike me down from
   above with a bolt from the blue.

(He darts an anxious glance upwards.)

AHMED: That's very interesting, Norm. But don't you
   feel that despite your heroic act, the barbarity of war
   left a scar on you?

NORM: Not a stratch. Of course, I was lucky, luckier
   than my old man. He was in the Gallipoli campaign –
   one of the original Anzacs.

(Pause.)

He fell at Lone Pine.

(Pause.)

It was a dawn raid. He was killed by a stray bullet. They buried him the same morning.

AHMED: I'm very sorry to hear that.

NORM: Well, that's the way it goes. After all, the price of liberty is eternal vigilance.

AHMED: The price of what?

NORM: Liberty.

AHMED: Oh.

(Pause.)

NORM: You're not having a go at me are you?

AHMED: No, not at all. I feel sorry for the Anzacs, poor fellows. However, the Anzac legend is often invoked in support of . . . other campaigns. But, forgive me, I am once again posing as a critic of your country. I must remember that I am a visitor to this land. A thousand apologies.

NORM: That's all right, Ahmed. You've got your views and I respect them. Long as you do the right thing by yourself and other blokes and don't go throwing your weight around, you'll be all right out here.

AHMED: Thank you, Norm, that is very good advice.

NORM: Don't mention it, Ahmed. I like to see blokes like you getting on well out here. All you Asian students coming out here to study and then going back to your own countries, it's a good thing, I reckon. Should be more of it. Mind you, though, not everyone goes along with it. A bloke at work said he didn't see the point of bringing a whole lot of boongs out here. Excuse the term, Ahmed, I'm just giving you a verbatim report, like, of what the bloke at work said. But I had occasion to take him to task when I heard him say that, Ahmed, I said 'We're forging the bonds of friendship with our Asian neighbours. Knowledge is the key to the door of understanding and friendship' – that's what I told him.

AHMED: That's very interesting Norm. But what specific course does this understanding and friendship take?

NORM: Well, you know . . . understanding . . . and . . . being friendly.

AHMED: I see.

NORM: (*quickly*) Anyway, Ahmed, what do you do in your spare time? Got any hobbies, play any sport?

AHMED: No I don't really have time for that sort of thing.

NORM: *No time for sport??* Jees, that's a sad state of affairs. I always used to find time to play sport when I was a young feller. I used to play football before the war. Rugby League. I played lock. That was my position, lock. Talk about cover defence! I used to hit 'em hard and low, round the knees, down they went. They can't run without legs, can they? That was my philosophy. But I was always a clean player, Ahmed, I never put the boot in. Always played hard and clean, I was a good sportsman, too. Never sold the dump to a mate. I always played fair, but if they ever mucked me about, biff! Send for the cleaners. All over bar the shouting. Know what I mean? I remember one bloke. A real coot. Played prop for Balmain juniors. Tall bloke, he was. A long thin streak of pelican shit. He tried to hang one on me at Leichhardt Oval once, so I administered a knuckle sandwich to him. He woke up in Our Lady of Mercy Hospital. Should have known better; I always observed the true spirit of the game. Ever played Rugby League, Ahmed?

AHMED: No, unfortunately. I have to spend most of my time studying.

NORM: That's a pity. It's not healthy, you know, to keep your nose stuck in a book all the time.

AHMED: Oh, I don't spend all my time studying. I am compelled to work at night to put myself through university.

NORM: Yeah? Why doesn't your old man send you a few bob to help you along? You wouldn't have to flog your chops too much then.

AHMED: My father is unable to supply me with financial assistance as he, unlike some other people, is not very affluent.

NORM: Jees, that's a bit rough. You've got my sympathy, Ahmed. You must have a pretty tough job, having to work and study at the same time.

AHMED: It is not easy.

NORM: What are you going to do when you finish?

AHMED: When I obtain my degree I intend to return to Pakistan and attempt to render assistance to the under-privileged peoples, perhaps also to undermine the position of the over-privileged peoples. I have some old school friends over there who are dedicated to the cause. I remember when I graduated from secondary school in Pakistan we had a speech day at the end of the year. It was an official ceremony, too, with all the, er, dignitaries, as you say out here. All the top civil servants and military men and businessmen were there on the official dais with the school authorities. As the highlight of the occasion it was arranged that a flock of doves would be released by the big window and would fly out over the playing fields of the school as some sort of symbolic gesture. But unfortunately they took fright at all the lights and the applause and suffered severe indigestion. They flew round and round and round above the dignitaries, bestowing excrement on the Establishment. We all laughed and laughed and some of the boys threw paper darts at the dignitaries. When one boy introduced a fire hose into the proceedings, the situation grew somewhat out of hand. I shall always cherish the memory I have of one bespattered military gentleman crawling around under a table trying to find one of his medals, as the gentle rain from heaven fell all around him. We boys had a great time. It was a mad, wild, exhilarating day, I shall always remember it.

(NORM *has been sitting on the handrail during this speech.
Now he stands.*)

NORM: Yeah, it sounds like a real rort. But, if you don't
mind my saying so, Ahmed, in a spirit of friendly
criticism, with no malice of forethought, or any
offence intended on my part, don't you think your
behaviour was a bit on the rough side? I mean, you
know, I'd be the last bloke to start defending the
bloody dignitaries, and I don't go much on pomp and
circumstance and all that sort of garbage, but still, all
in all, and looking at both sides of the question, I'd be
a bit inclined to say that the blokes who get into these
official positions, well, they're pretty important
blokes, and I'd say they deserve a little bit of respect
from the general public. I mean, I'd be the last one to
start putting them up on a pedestal, and if they ever
bung on side with me, mate, they know what they can
expect. I don't take no crap from no one. But, by the
same token, and taking all things into consideration, I
reckon that if a bloke's in an official capacity, like
those blokes who came to your school, well, it's only
fair that he should earn a little bit of respect.

AHMED: I fear I must disagree with you there, Norm.
I do not regard these accursed officials with perhaps
the same reverence as you do. We shall overthrow
them! We demand social justice! Oh, I beg your
pardon, Norm, I fear I was carried away there for a
moment. I hope you will excuse my excessive zeal.

NORM: Ar, she's right, Ahmed. But just remember
what I said. Anyway, I hope you get through uni all
right, so you can go back to your country and do whatever it is you want to do. As a matter of fact, I've got a
son at uni. Young Bernie. He's studying in America.
He's at the M.I.T. – the Massachusetts Institute of
Technology.

AHMED: What's he studying?

NORM: Well . . . technology, you know? He's got an
assured future in front of him, my Bernie, he'll be a
leader in science and industry – he's got the qualifica-

tions, you see. He's a real cluey bloke, no risk. We were very proud of him when he graduated from Sydney Uni. It was an official ceremony. All the dignitaries were there . . . the Governor, the Premier and the Governor-General, all up there on the official dais with all the other authorities. What a magnificent sight! Bernie wasn't nervous. He came through fine. It was a very impressive ceremony.

AHMED: It must have been a proud moment for you, Norm.

NORM: Yes, it certainly was. Bernie's the only one in our family with a university degree. None of the rest of us are all that bright. But the Gallaghers are getting on, mate. My old man was a factory worker, I'm a white-collar worker, and now Bernie's a technologist. Things are looking up, I tell you.

AHMED: What kind of white-collar work do you do, Norm?

NORM: Well, er, actually I'm a storeman, like, in a warehouse. But I wear a white shirt and tie under me dustcoat, though. I mean, I'm not sort of technically a white-collar worker, but I wear a white collar, y'see? I mean, there's a bit of a fine distinction involved in this. Y'see, I'm not always in the warehouse – I spend a lot of time in the office, checking invoices and rectifying a few anomalies.

AHMED: Ah, I see. It sounds very complicated.

NORM: Yes, it's a funny business. But I'm doing all right for meself. Making a bit of money, got a nice big house, everything laid on, I'm doing fine. But there's just one thing wrong, Ahmed.

AHMED: What's that?

NORM: Well, you see, Ahmed, I'm all alone now, since my good wife Beryl passed away to the heavens above.

AHMED: I'm very sorry to hear that, Norm, you must be rather lonely.

NORM: That I am, Ahmed, that I am. Sometimes when I'm out in the backyard, watering the frangipannis, I feel very lonely, I really do. Now that dear Beryl's in

another world I don't know where I am. She was a
lovely woman, a real beauty in her day. Jet-black hair,
sparkling eyes, and an ear for music. Played a good
game of bowls in her twilight years. But now she's
gone and where am I? Up the creek without a paddle!
It's the good times I miss, Ahmed, those magic
moments that make life seem worthwhile. Like the
time we danced all night at the Bronte R.S.L. Yes I
really miss dear old Beryl, with her happy laugh, her
way with kids, her curried eggs on toast of a winter's
night. But now, Ahmed, now I sit at home alone and
think of yesteryear.

AHMED: That is most unfortunate, Norm. But surely
you must have some human contact, some form of
social intercourse?

NORM: Oh yeah, my daughter Lorraine comes round
and cooks me roast dinner of a Sunday. But she's
married, you see, she's got her own life to lead. She
made a good catch, that girl. Got on to a real go-
ahead type. Young Gary. He's in the retail business,
you know. Runs a hot dog stand at Harold Park. Got
his eye on a kiosk at Miranda. No flies on Gary, mate,
you mark my words. Fine looking young feller, too.
Very tall, with big broad shoulders and a good head
for figures. Likes a dash of lemon in his Resch's. He
comes around and takes me out to the football sometimes. I get a little lonely, you see, being all alone. I
like to get out and do something, meet some people. I
like to have a nice chat with a bloke, find out how he's
getting on in the world. A bloke like you, for instance,
Ahmed. A visitor to our shores. A young citizen from
the south-east Asian sub-continent.

AHMED: Well . . . I hope I can . . . I mean . . . if I can
be of . . . any . . . that is, I . . .

NORM: Step over here a minute, will you?

(Pause.)

AHMED: What?

(They look at each other.)

NORM: Just step over here for a minute.

(Pause.)
AHMED: Why?
NORM: What's the matter, Ahmed? Come here.
(AHMED *moves warily closer to* NORM.)
   Over here. Under the light.
(AHMED *moves closer.*)
AHMED: What do you want?
(NORM *surveys* AHMED.)
NORM: Just as I thought.
(Pause.)
   You haven't really got such a dark skin, have you?
AHMED: A dark skin? What do you mean?
NORM: I mean you're not a black, are you? You could
   pass for a Greek or a Turk. You've got more of an
   olive complexion.
AHMED: What are you getting at? I fail to under-
   stand . . .
(NORM *laughs. He moves out from the shadows.*)
NORM: Don't get upset, Ahmed. Don't do your block.
   I was only thinking that if you didn't have a dark skin
   you'd be all right. I mean, it'd be all right for you to
   stay here, like, get a job and stay in this country. But
   you haven't really got a dark skin, have you? It's sort
   of olive coloured. They'd never call you 'Mr. Midnight', would they?
AHMED: Some would.
NORM: Eh, come on Ahmed, now don't have a wetty.
   No offence meant. You're not angry, are you? Eh?
AHMED: No, it's all right, Norm, I'm not offended.
NORM: Good. We're still mates, then. I suppose you'd
   have a right to get touchy about that sort of thing. I
   wouldn't blame you for getting touchy. I can see your
   point of view.
AHMED: Thank you, Norm. I appreciate your concern.
NORM: She's right, Ahmed. I tell you what, in this
   world we've got to learn to understand the problems
   of others and not worry too much about our own.
AHMED: That is very true, Norm. You seem to possess
   a most humanitarian outlook on life.

NORM: I'm very flattered, Ahmed, to hear you say that. In this world there's too many blokes getting in for their chop and not worrying about their mates. You'd appreciate that, I mean, being a historian and all.

AHMED: Uh, yes, I suppose I would.

NORM: You know, as I was saying, Ahmed, you could do all right for yourself if you stayed out here. After you got your degree, you could stay here and be a useful asset. I mean, as I said, you're not really black, so you wouldn't have that much trouble.

AHMED: Well, perhaps. I shall have to obtain my degree before I consider a proposal of that nature.

NORM: That's fair enough. First things first, after all. But give it a bit of thought, Ahmed. You'd be welcome out here, I can vouch for that. The people'd treat you just like one of their own, no risk. You'd be all right. No worries there. You could make your way in the world out here.

AHMED: Yes, it is a most attractive proposition.

NORM: You could have a good time out here, Ahmed. It's an easy life. Take this morning, for instance. On Sunday mornings I sit out on the terrace and sip a Tia Maria and read the sports section. Lorraine's in the kitchen, smell of a roast lamb on the breeze, what more could you want? Green lawns all around, vista of the harbour, Holden in the garage, I'm sweet. No worries. See what I'm getting at? You wouldn't have that in Pakistan, now would you? You could set yourself up very nicely out here. There's lots to recommend it, believe you me. It's a bloody good set-up, take my tip. Look at me. I've got a good job, good pay – I'm doing all right. A reliable firm, nice personnel. You know who I had a beer with on Friday?

AHMED: No, Norm, I have no idea. Who?

NORM: I had a beer with the man himself, the managing director, my boss. *(Filled with awe)* I drank with the managing director of the firm.

AHMED: That must have been ... an experience.

NORM: He shouted a round, too, just like any ordinary bloke would. He took a shine to me, too, I could see that. He was very impressed with me. It was a most cordial affair. I know how to conduct meself on these occasions. Not like my old man. Do you know what he had?

AHMED: What?

NORM: He had a criminal record. It's true. My mother told me. He was put away for a while.

AHMED: What did he do?

NORM: He bashed up his boss. Yes, that's right, bashed up his boss. It's . . . inconceivable, that's what it is. Talk about a blot on the family record. It's a stain on the Gallagher escutcheon. The memory of it still haunts me. It's enough to make you want to chuck, isn't it? Course, you wouldn't find that sort of thing around these days. Rare as a pregnant nun. That's progress for you. We've cut that sort of thing out.

AHMED: Yes, it would indeed be a rare occurrence in contemporary times.

NORM: Too right. Yes, he was a real ratbag, my old man. Mad Dan Gallagher, they used to call him. Always getting into fights and organizing strikes and things. He died just before I was born. My mother nearly had a miscarriage when she heard the news, but she got over it all right. I arrived safe and sound. She used to tell me about him when I was a young feller. He was always holding meetings in our living room. Then they'd all go into the kitchen and my mother would make them a cup of tea. All big men they were, with horny hands and sturdy braces. My mother was real tiny. They'd pick her up and whirl her round and round and round the room and when they were drunk they'd sing *I'll Take You Home Again, Kathleen* or *The Wild Colonial Boy*. There was a whole mob of them – Flanigan, Hanigan, Branigan, Lanigan, O'Toole, O'Riley and Schultz. Then one night the cops raided the place and took them away. They were

all singing *Sweet Adeline* in the Black Maria. What a
bunch of ratbags they were! Some of them used to
come round after the war to see my mother. I was only
a kid then. They gave me some licorice. We lost touch
with them after a while. It was a bit before my time,
all that. I got dim memories . . . like . . . long time
ago . . . bit cloudy . . . Wobbly bastards!

(NORM *kicks over the garbage can in a fit of anger.* AHMED
is a bit startled, but doesn't move.)

Jees, there I go again, doing me block. Excuse me,
Ahmed, but my old man does make me angry. He had
no respect for law and order and common decency.

AHMED: Perhaps it is sometimes desirable to effect an
alteration in the status quo.

NORM: Could be. But my old man wanted to change
things, Ahmed, he tried to buck the system. You can't
do that.

AHMED: Not in this country, at any rate.

NORM: No fear. Anyway, they got on to him pretty
quick. The policemen came around and took him
away, but not before he'd bashed one of them up. An
officer of the law. Disgraceful! It's like I told you, he
had no respect for law and order, and that's a terrible
thing.

AHMED: Oh, I don't know, sometimes I feel the police
deserve some form of retaliation from their victims.

NORM: Ar, come on, Ahmed, give the copper a fair go.
They're not such bad blokes. Give them a break.
They're just doing their job, that's all. They only
want to preserve law and order in the community.
Mind you, though, if a mug copper ever started
pushing me around, I'd job him good and proper, no
risk about that. I don't take no crap from no one. But,
by the same token, Ahmed, I reckon our policemen
are doing a pretty good job and I'd do all that's in my
power, all that's humanly possible to assist them in the
performance of their duties. Go easy on the old
wallopers, that's what I say, give the coppers a fair go.

AHMED: Well, I think they get a pretty fair go. I

observed one beating up an old drunk earlier this evening. For no reason, either. It was sheer brutality.

NORM: Now come on, Ahmed, the policemen do a good job keeping all the drunks and pervs off the streets and making them safe for decent citizens. These blokes are a menace, you know, especially the pervs. Ever been solicited, Ahmed?

AHMED: No, I have not been accorded that distinction.

NORM: Well, you want to watch out for that sort of thing. It could happen anytime.

AHMED: Yes, I'm certain it could.

NORM: Yes, anytime, any time at all. Pervs aren't choosy, you know. Some of these blokes'll drop their tweeds for a ripe banana. I saw an old perv in Centennial Park last week. He was having a tug in the gutter, going at it hammer and tongs. He must have been hard up, eh?

AHMED: Uh . . . yes.

NORM: You ever get like that, Ahmed? Eh? Do you?

AHMED: No.

NORM: Never get hard up?

AHMED: No.

NORM: Never had a tug in the gutter?

AHMED: Certainly not. I hardly think a public thoroughfare is a suitable venue for conducting autonomous experiments of that nature.

(Pause.)

NORM: You got a funny way of putting things, Ahmed.

AHMED: You find my syntax humorous?

NORM: No, not humorous, Ahmed. Just funny. I suppose you get a lot of people who admit you speak better than they do, eh? I bet a lot of people say you speak better than the average native-born Australian.

AHMED: Yes, I have been paid that compliment.

NORM: Yes, I could very well . . . envisage that. But anyway, Ahmed, that's just another reason why you should settle down out here – there's no language barrier. You could live here very . . . autonomously. You're not like all those chows down in Dixon Street that jabber away in Chinese half the time. You can speak the Queen's English. You know, you could really make something of yourself if you stayed out here, Ahmed. Look at my boss, for instance.

AHMED: That managing director fellow?

NORM: Yes. He was telling me about the struggles he's had to establish his great enterprise. It wasn't easy, he said, in the early days. It was hard at first, but he won through in the end. It was a stirring struggle, but one man's dream came true. He became a legend in his own lifetime. He challenged the gods and carved out a name for himself that will survive in the anals of human endeavour. But that's the sort of thing that happens in this country, Ahmed. You could have a success story like that, you know. Start off with a billy-cart and finish up with a fleet of Boeing 727s.

AHMED: Perhaps. I have not given much thought to –

NORM: You could settle down, get a house in a nice suburb with lots of trees and birds and things. A place where you can wash the car of a Saturday and do a bit of gardening of a Sunday. Do you like gardening, Ahmed?

AHMED: It is indeed a pleasant pastime. I like to –

NORM: That's for sure. There's nothing I like better than to get out in the garden of a Sunday. Put me amongst the hydrangeas and I'm at peace with the world. When there's a breeze in the palms and the sun's getting low, I get out in the yard and get stuck into the weeds. I weed away to my heart's content. I couldn't ask for any more in this world or the next, and that's my solemn oath. It's the simple pleasures, Ahmed, that make this life worth living. Sometimes when I'm on my way home from church of a Sunday night, when the strains of the last hymn have died and the humble pilgrims have gone home to bed, I stop and look up at the stars in the sky and think what a wonderful world it is we live in. But, by the same token, Ahmed, I do miss the old days a bit. The times when we used to sit around the fire with our friends and sing all night. There was real warmth between people in those days. We were like brothers, all getting stuck into the grog together. And when I was out in the bush and I stopped at a pub, I knew every bloke in the place within five minutes. Community feeling, that's what it was, community feeling. We used to have it in the old days. And when I sit home of a night, all by myself, I open a can of D.A. and think back over my life. The happy, happy times, like when the young fellers started calling on Lorraine. She was a lovely girl. Dead spit of Beryl, she was. She – ar jees, Ahmed, look, I'm sorry to carry on like this. I don't known what you must think.

AHMED: Oh, no, Norm, you go right ahead.

NORM: Sorry to crap on so much, Ahmed. I don't know what came over me. It's just that I don't get much of a chance to talk to people these days. And I do like a bit of a yarn, I really do. Just to talk to someone, that's all I want. And when I do find some-one to talk to, I just mag away like an old woman and ruin everything.

AHMED: You say whatever you want to, Norm, I don't mind.

NORM: I just crap on and spoil it all.

AHMED: No you don't, Norm. I have been listening, believe me.

NORM: You mean that, Ahmed?

AHMED: Of course I mean it.

NORM: Good on you, Ahmed, you're a real human being. I don't suppose it's easy to put up with an old bludger like me.

AHMED: On the contrary, Norm, it has been most interesting to meet you.

NORM: Thanks, old mate, that's very nice of you, to say that. Well, I'd better let you go now, Ahmed. But just before you go, I would like to say this from the very bottom of my heart, that I wish you every success in the world. And I do hope you get on well out here. Now you're sure you're settling down all right?

AHMED: Oh yes, I'm making my way.

NORM: I'm glad to hear it, Ahmed. I wouldn't like to think of you as being lonely. You see, I'm on my own, too, and I know what it's like. A young bloke your age ought to be out and about, mixing with people, getting amongst the girls. You know what your trouble is, Ahmed, don't you?

AHMED: What?

NORM: You're too shy. That's the first thing I noticed about you. You're too shy.

AHMED: You think so?

NORM: Of course. It's obvious.

AHMED: It is true that I do not have many friends.

NORM: Look, I tell you what, Ahmed. Why don't you go up to the New South Wales Leagues' Club and have a good time. Mention my name to the bloke on the door and you'll be in like the proverbial Flynn. Just tell 'em Norm sent you, that's all you have to do. Go up with your mates and get on the hops. You'll soon get to know the blokes up there. A great mob they are, too. I've got a feeling they'll take to you, Ahmed, I think you'll go down well.

AHMED: Thank you, Norm, I shall bear that in mind.

NORM: You do that, Ahmed, you do that. I'd like to see you meeting some people, making some friends. Loneliness is a terrible curse, Ahmed, and I'd like to see you coming out of your shell. We're not such a bad mob out here, you know. We might be a bit on the rough-and-ready side, but our heart's in the right place.

AHMED: Oh, I have had ample proof of that.

NORM: And as I said, Ahmed, you really ought to give a thought to staying out here. Find yourself a good woman, something more than just a weekend root, and settle down and raise a family. Buy a weekender on the coast, join the local leagues' club – ever been to a leagues' club, Ahmed?

AHMED: No, I have that pleasure in front of me.

NORM: Fabulous places. They've improved a lot, these clubs. Twenty years ago they weren't much chop, just a place to go when you wanted to get out on the grog. But now, jees, what a difference! They go in for amenities a lot these days, for the comfort of the patrons. They're very well appointed, these clubs, very well appointed. Anyway, Ahmed, there it is. Good prospects, you could have a good time, what more could you ask for? This place'd be made for a bloke like you.

AHMED: Well, I think I will concentrate on completing my tertiary education first. My primary concern is to obtain a liberal education and my secondary concern is to gain a deeper understanding of human behaviour.

NORM: Ah . . . yes, that's fair enough. But keep it in mind, Ahmed, we'd love to have you. And the people – they'd take you to their hearts. Everyone from Alice Springs to breakfast time. It'll be a red carpet job.

AHMED: Thank you very much, Norm, that is very nice of you. I must say I have received some warm hospitality from a lot of people since I have been in your country. It has been most gratifying. Of course, uh, not everyone has extended this hospitality towards visitors from eastern backgrounds, such as myself.

NORM: Ar well, you've got to take the rough with the smooth. There's ratbags wherever you go. But the majority of people'll do the right thing. I think you'll go down well out here.

AHMED: Thank you again, Norm. I certainly hope so. You have given me something to think about.

NORM: Glad to hear it. Well, Ahmed, I must say it's been a pleasure to meet you and have this little talk. I mean, to reach a common understanding. That's what the world needs, I reckon, a bit of common understanding.

AHMED: That is very true. I have enjoyed meeting you, too, Norm, it has been a real pleasure.

NORM: Put 'er there, mate.
(He offers his hand.)
AHMED: *(reaching out to shake hands)* Yes, I –
(NORM *punches* AHMED *in the stomach, then in the face.*
He grabs AHMED's *head and bashes it against the post.*
Then he flings the limp body over the handrail.)
NORM: Fuckin' boong.
(The clock strikes one.)

BLACKOUT

Max Phipps as Bentley in the Nimrod Street Theatre production of *Rooted*, Sydney 1972, directed by Ken Horler. Photo: Anthony Horler.

Rooted

BENTLEY
SANDY
GARY
RICHARD
DIANE

All the characters are in their mid-twenties.

SCENE

Sydney, over a period of ten weeks.

ACT I: *The living room of* BENTLEY *and* SANDY's *home unit.*

ACT II: *The same.*

ACT III: RICHARD's *studio.*

Rooted was first performed simultaneously on 14th August 1969 by Stage at the Childers Street Hall, Canberra and at the Jane Street Theatre, Sydney, with the following casts, respectively:

BENTLEY	Bruce Widdop
SANDY	Karin Altmann
GARY	Clive Scollay
RICHARD	Philip Wheeler
DIANE	Peta Adams

Setting designed by Jon Stephens

Directed by Allan Mawer

BENTLEY	Jeff Kevin
SANDY	Pat Bishop
GARY	Gregory Ross
RICHARD	Garry McDonald
DIANE	Sandy Gore

Setting designed by Kevin Carpenter

Directed by Rick Billinghurst

Act One

SCENE ONE

Saturday night. The living room of BENTLEY *and* SANDY's *home unit. The room is white and all the furniture is white, except for two armchairs, which are blue. The furniture is very modern. There is a door, down R., and a passageway, up L. There is one window in the right wall upstage. There is a sideboard along the right wall, a stereo set against the back wall and a cabinet against the left wall. The walls are bare. On the sideboard there is a tape recorder, a transistor radio, and a telephone.*

BENTLEY and SANDY's *house-warming party has just finished and the room is littered with beer-cans, glasses, full ashtrays etc.* BENTLEY *and* SANDY *are posing for a photograph by the sideboard, and* GARY *is holding a camera. He moves around, looking for a good position.*

GARY: Say cheese.
BENTLEY: Cheese.
GARY: Got it.
BENTLEY: Let's have another one, over by the stereo set.
GARY: Righto.
BENTLEY: How's this?
(They pose by the stereo set.)
GARY: Say cheese.
BENTLEY: Cheese.
GARY: Got it.
BENTLEY: Let's have another one over –
SANDY: That's enough!
BENTLEY: All right, darling. Whatever you say. Like another beer, Gary?
GARY: I wouldn't mind. Just a nogginette, thanks.
(SANDY sits down, looking tired and irritated. BENTLEY pours GARY a beer.)
BENTLEY: Chug-a-lug.
GARY: Chug-a-lug.

29

BENTLEY: How did you think the turn went?

GARY: It was a beauty. Best house-warming party I've been to.

BENTLEY: What do you think of the unit?

GARY: Immaculate. Bloody immaculate.

BENTLEY: You hear that, Sandy? Gary reckons our unit's immaculate.

SANDY: Yes, I heard.

GARY: You must have paid a pretty fair price for it.

BENTLEY: Well, they're not giving them away.

GARY: You must be doing all right for yourself, Bentley.

BENTLEY: Ar, not too bad. You think everyone enjoyed themselves tonight?

GARY: Oh yeah. It was a great turn.

BENTLEY: You hear that, Sandy? Gary reckons it was a great turn.

SANDY: Yes, I heard.

GARY: Davo got stuck into the grog, didn't he?

BENTLEY: Bloody Davo. Jees I had to laugh. Nearly went off my face.

GARY: You see Davo cracking on? First bird he's had in ages.

BENTLEY: Ar well, better than his right hand, I suppose.

GARY: Old Davo certainly enjoyed himself.

BENTLEY: You hear that, Sandy? Gary reckons Davo enjoyed himself.

SANDY: Yes, I heard.

GARY: I liked the records you played tonight, Bentley.

BENTLEY: Did you?

GARY: Yeah, bloody good music.

BENTLEY: You think everyone liked the music?

GARY: Oh yeah. Diane went off her brain.

BENTLEY: Did she ever!

GARY: That's a great stereo set you got there, Bentley.

BENTLEY: You hear that, Sandy?

SANDY: Gary reckons we've got a great stereo set.

BENTLEY: Yes, I heard.

SANDY: Do you two know what time it is?
BENTLEY: *(looking at watch)* Jees, it's a quarter to three.
SANDY: That's right.
GARY: I'd better be going.
SANDY: Yes.
GARY: Getting a bit late.
SANDY: It's a quarter to three.
GARY: Yes, I heard.
BENTLEY: One for the road?
SANDY: It's getting a bit late.
GARY: I'd better be going. See you later.
(BENTLEY *opens the door.* GARY *goes over.*)
BENTLEY: Send us the photos when they're ready.
GARY: Will do. Going down the beach tomorrow?
SANDY: Goodnight, Gary.
GARY: Goodnight.
(GARY *exits.* BENTLEY *starts clearing up the room.*
SANDY *sits back in the armchair and closes her eyes.*)
BENTLEY: Are you tired, darling?
SANDY: Yes. It's getting a bit late.
BENTLEY: I'm a bit buggered myself. Enjoy the party?
SANDY: Yes.
BENTLEY: Everyone had a good time, I think.
Especially Simmo.
(BENTLEY *takes some glasses and ashtrays out to the kitchen
on a tray. He re-enters and tidies up.*)
Everyone raved about the unit, didn't they? Mind
you, this is only a stepping stone. When I get to grade
ten we'll have a villa at Bayview and a cruiser at
Pittwater.
(He continues tidying up, then stops.)
Oh, uh, by the way, darling, there was one thing I
meant to say to you.
(Pause.)
What was it? Well, I'll tell you, darling. You see, I
noticed Simmo paying you a lot of attention tonight.
He left the keg twice to talk to you. So I sort of took
him aside and said: 'Look, Simmo, I know you're a
big mover with the birds, but Sandy's my wife, so I'd

just like to sort of . . . ascertain your intentions . . . as
it were.'
(Pause.)
He told me to get stuffed.
(Pause.)
Huh. Funny bloke, Simmo. You want to watch out
for him. Still, I know there's nothing in it.
(Pause.)
I wouldn't get . . . involved with Simmo, if I were you.
(Pause.)
Still, I know there's nothing in it.
(Pause. He continues tidying up.)
Yes, everyone had a good time tonight. Diane went
off her brain.
(He continues tidying up as he speaks.)
Everyone raved about the unit. And the stereo set.
(He dusts the stereo set.)
Yes, it was a great turn.
(He looks at SANDY.*)*
Well, that's that. Ready for bed?
*(*SANDY *is asleep.)*
Fast asleep. Poor darling. You're worn out.
(He looks at her.)
You're beautiful, you know that? The blokes've
always reckoned I've hit the jackpot. Especially Davo.
(He picks her up.)
Come on, beddy byes.
(He carries her out.)
Beddy byes, darling.
(He carries her into the bedroom and closes the door.)

FADE OUT

SCENE TWO

Sunday afternoon, one week later. BENTLEY *sits in a chair reading the Sunday
paper. The audience can't see his face. There is an ironing board and an iron at the
back of the room. Silence for a while, then* SANDY *rushes in, wearing a short slip
and carrying a black dress. As she talks, she irons a wet spot on the dress, and puts it
on later in her speech.*

SANDY: *(loudly and quickly)* This damn dress! It's still got a mark on it. I took it to the dry cleaners around the corner the other day and they said they'd get it off all right. It'd be no trouble for them, they said, have it off in no time without any trace they said. Then I came back the next day to pick it up and the spot was still there so I really got MAD and told off the old bitch something terrible. Funny looking little woman she was, too – raven hair, eyes like a hawk, and pigeon toes. Walked with a squint and spoke like a Greek – I think she was an Italian Jew with German blood. So then she asked me what the stain was and I said beer. I said I was at this party and a CREEP called Davo spilt his drink in my lap and wet me right through and caused this big stain and you haven't got it out yet, what do you mean by calling yourselves dry cleaners it's a FRAUD. I said I'm going out on Sunday night and I went to look my best so you'd better do something about it but QUICK. That's what I told the old bitch and she said you'd better speak to the manager and took me back through the curtains to the office where this real old man was sitting behind a plastic desk with an eye shade and it looked like it was her husband – I mean he had that look about him. Jet black hair falling out with glasses and a beard. SO-O-O, then I said to him you've got a nerve what do you mean by saying you're dry cleaners when you can't even get a beer stain off my dress when I've got a date on Sunday night and want to look my best. Oh yes, he said, I remember we had the same trouble with Rebecca Rosenberg's grey slack suit. BUGGER Rebecca Rosenberg's grey slack suit I said what about my little black dress I've got a date on Sunday so DO something about it. Oooo, he said with a wrinkle in his eye, have you got yourself a boyfriend. Yes I said and I'm going out with him on Sunday night so you'd better have this dress ready in time. Oooo, he said with another wrinkle what's your boyfriend like, a nice respectable fellow. Yes I said as a matter of fact he's one of my husband's best friends. Then we got down to business and he said he'd see to it personally and come back tomorrow but when I came back tomorrow it still had a stain on it so I went back and told him and he said he was sorry with a shrug. SORRY I said look sweetheart I've got a date with Simmo on Sunday and I want to look my best so get to work on it. Simmo he said well why didn't you say you had a date with Simmo I'd have seen to it personally. SO then he took it and said come back in half an hour so I came back and it was in a plastic bag and he winked at me with his glass eye and said all was well now dear. BUT I ripped it off before his very eyes and the stain was still there on the dress so I threw it back in his face. If you don't get it out I'll get Simmo on to you I said. You should have seen him MOVE. He said come back in an hour and scuttled away with the dress and when I came back he gave it to me in another plastic bag and I said no tricks and he said no it was all right now. BUT when I got home and opened the bag it still had a stain on it I could have cried. I've tried petrol, lighter fluid, metho and kero but it won't come off so I'll just have to hope Simmo doesn't notice it.

(A car horn is heard.)

Oh there's Simmo now. I'll have to fly. There's some corned beef in the fridge.

(She rushes out the front door. BENTLEY *lowers his paper and looks after her.)*

FADE OUT

SCENE THREE

Sunday afternoon, one week later. Lights up on SANDY, *who is sitting in an armchair cleaning and filing her nails. After a little while,* BENTLEY *comes in the front door. He is wearing tennis whites and carries a racquet. In his other hand he carries a small trophy. He stands, watching* SANDY. *She appears not to notice him. Silence.*

BENTLEY: We won.
(Pause.)
Huh. We won the doubles cup.
(He holds up the trophy. Pause. He puts it on the sideboard.)
They took us to five sets.
(Pause.)
Whew!
(Silence. BENTLEY takes a tennis ball out of his pocket and bounces it up and down on his racquet. This goes on for a little while and he gets quite wrapped up in it. SANDY looks up and starts watching him. He keeps it going while he reaches into his pocket and brings out another ball. He gets two of them going at once. He manages this at first, but soon he is trying desperately to keep them both going. Finally, both balls fall to the floor. BENTLEY and SANDY watch the balls bounce and then roll to a standstill. Silence. SANDY resumes filing her nails.)
I went for a walk this morning. Down to the beach. Very early, it was. You were still asleep. I went down to the promenade. You know the promenade? Had a squint at the old Pacific. I walked along the promenade. Just walked along to the end there, to the rocks. You know the rocks? I stood on the rocks and looked at the sea. Very fresh, what with the salty air and the sea breeze and all. The old Pacific. What an ocean! What an ocean. Sparkling. There was a bit of mist about. Not much, just a bit. Then I walked around the headland, round a bit further where it juts out. There was a small rock pool there. I discovered it, quite by accident. A small rock pool, all by itself. A bit of sea that got left behind by the tide. The water was clear, very clear. You could see the odd grain of sand on the bottom. There was no one about, so I took a quick dip in the pool. Stripped down, hopped in, splashed about, lovely. Lovely. I lay on my back and floated along. Not a ripple. You couldn't hear a sound. I floated for quite a while, till the sun came out on the water. Sparkling. Then the mist lifted and I heard voices, so I got dressed and climbed back down to the promenade. It was sunny now, people around, splashing in the sand.

There was sunlight splattered all over the place. All
over the sea, all over the sand, all over me. Sunlight
everywhere. Sparkling. Then I came back here. You
were still asleep. I looked at you. Like a baby.
(Pause.)
It was a beautiful walk.
(Pause.)
Down there by the old Pacific. It really is a magnifi-
cent ocean, you know. Goes for miles.
(Pause.)
I tell you what, why don't we go for a swim?
(Pause.)
Let's hop in the B and fang up to the beach. We could
go up the coast and down an ale at the Arms.
(Pause.)
Might bump into Davo up there. He's been known to
bend an elbow at the Arms.
(Pause.)
What do you say?
(Pause.)
About this thing with Simmo, darling. You're not . . .
sort of . . . you know . . .
(Pause.)
I'd like to have a little talk to you about this thing
with Simmo.
(Pause.)
Let's have a drink and talk it over, eh?
*(He goes to the sideboard and brings out a large glass bowl half
filled with blue liquid, the same colour as the armchairs.)*
I knocked off the punch from the turn last night. Did
you have any? It was put there for the birds. Sort of a
female keg. Like some?
(He gets two glasses and scoops out some punch.)
There you are. Do you good.
(He drinks, then winces.)
Jees, bloody potent stuff, this. Fair knocks you. Davo
tipped a bottle of Gilbey's into it. Laced it for openers.
That was the secret of his success last night. She never
knew what hit her.

(Pause.)

Go on, have a bit. Goes down well. You'll enjoy it.

(Pause.)

Brushes away the cobwebs.

(Pause.)

About this thing with Simmo . . .

(Pause.)

I bought some new stuff on Friday. Look at this little transistor. Latest model. Japanese. I also bought a tape recorder. Beauty, isn't it? They don't give these things away, you know. I'll show you how it works.

(He switches it on and speaks into the microphone.)

Testing 1-2-3.

(He switches to playback, but SANDY's voice is heard on the tape.)

SANDY'S VOICE: Why don't you shut up?

(BENTLEY's jaw drops. He switches off the tape recorder, looks at SANDY, then looks at the machine. He is disconcerted.)

BENTLEY: Huh.

SANDY: Look, I tell you what.

BENTLEY: What?

SANDY: Why don't you move out? Huh? Why don't you pack up and get out?

BENTLEY: I can't.

SANDY: Why not?

BENTLEY: I live here.

SANDY: I know you live here. I've noticed you around the place from time to time. You know what you are, don't you?

BENTLEY: No.

SANDY: You're a ghost. That's what you are. You haunt this place. You haunt me. You're worse than Davo. Sometimes I wake up in the dead of the night and I can hear you moaning. It's creepy. I just don't want you around any more.

BENTLEY: But this is my home. This is my home unit.

SANDY: I know that. But why don't you find another one? Go somewhere else? I mean, I've got all sorts of things I want to do. I'm constantly on the move. But you never do anything. I mean, what do you do, you don't do anything, do you?

BENTLEY: I do . . . lots of things.

SANDY: What?

(Pause.)

BENTLEY: Lots of things.

SANDY: Let me put it in simple language: I want you to move out.

BENTLEY: Let me reply to you in equally simple language, darling: your proposal constitutes a violation of the legal rights of the duly authorised tenant of the said premises.

(Pause.)

SANDY: Anyway, you're annoying Simmo. You're getting on his nerves. I'm terribly sorry, but I must ask you to shoot through at your earliest possible convenience.

BENTLEY: But I live here.

SANDY: If you say that once more, I'll throw up.

BENTLEY: Sorry, darling.

SANDY: Look, if you don't move out, I'll get Simmo on to you.

BENTLEY: You wouldn't do that. You wouldn't do that to your own husband.

(He moves towards her.)

Now come on, darling. You're only kidding, aren't you?

(He tries to put his arm around her. She has resumed her nail filing and doesn't look up.)

SANDY: Get out of it.

(BENTLEY *retreats.*)

BENTLEY: Huh. Sorry, darling, I didn't meant to . . . disrupt . . .

(Pause.)

Anyway, you can't threaten me. No sir. You can't push me around. Huh! So what if you do go and tell him. Go ahead. I'm not scared. You tell him. Boy! Try to threaten me, eh? Huh!

(There is a knock on the door. BENTLEY jumps.)

SANDY: Answer it.
BENTLEY: What?
SANDY: Answer the door.
BENTLEY: You answer it.
SANDY: What?
BENTLEY: You answer the door.
SANDY: Get over there and open that door.
BENTLEY: What do you think I am? A bloody servant? I'm the boss around here and don't you forget it.
(Pause.)
I'm your kingpin.
(Pause.)
SANDY: Open . . . that . . . door.
(Pause.)
BENTLEY: All right, I'm going. What do I care?
(He moves towards the door.)
Doesn't worry me. I couldn't care less.
(He opens the door. RICHARD and DIANE come in. They are dressed very modishly. Silence.)
RICHARD: Hello, Bentley.
BENTLEY: Say, who are you?
RICHARD: Richard. Remember?
BENTLEY: Richard?
RICHARD: From school, remember?
BENTLEY: Oh, Richard!
RICHARD: That's right.
BENTLEY: Is that you?
RICHARD: Yes.
BENTLEY: Richard from school?
RICHARD: That's me.
BENTLEY: Richard!
RICHARD: Bentley.
BENTLEY: You've changed.
RICHARD: Yes.
BENTLEY: Richard!
RICHARD: Bentley.
BENTLEY: Old Richard, eh?
RICHARD: Yes.

BENTLEY: I can't believe it.
RICHARD: It's me all right.
BENTLEY: Richard!
RICHARD AND SANDY: Bentley!
(Pause.)
BENTLEY: Hello, Richard.
RICHARD: Hello, Bentley.
(Pause. He turns to SANDY.*)*
  Uh . . . hi.
BENTLEY: Oh sorry, I forgot. This is my wife Sandy.
(BENTLEY *turns to* SANDY.)
  This is Richard.
SANDY: Who?
RICHARD: How do you do?
SANDY: How do you do.
RICHARD: You know Diane.
BENTLEY: Hello, Diane.
DIANE: Hi.
(Pause.)
BENTLEY: Well, what a surprise!
RICHARD: Yes.
(Pause.)
BENTLEY: Haven't seen you for years.
RICHARD: No, must be . . . well, not since we left
  school.
(They smile awkwardly at each other.)
BENTLEY: What are you doing with yourself these
  days?
RICHARD: Oh, nothing much. What about you?
BENTLEY: Oh, I'm with the public service. Been there
  for years. Grade three now. Alan White reckons I'm a
  moral for grade four.
RICHARD: Yeah?
BENTLEY: It's a pretty soft cop. The money's good.
  Plenty of super.
RICHARD: Always one jump ahead, weren't you?
BENTLEY: Well, I always like to be able to be in a
  position where I can cope with any given exigency at
  any given time.

(SANDY *looks at him.*)

RICHARD: That's the stuff.

BENTLEY: Well, anyway, it's good to get together again.

RICHARD: Yeah.

(Pause.)

BENTLEY: Say, how did you know where to find me?

RICHARD: Davo told me.

BENTLEY: Old Davo, eh?

RICHARD: Yes. He said you were expecting Simmo this afternoon. He said Simmo was a frequent visitor here.

SANDY: That's right.

RICHARD: Good friends with Simmo, are you Bentley?

SANDY: I am.

RICHARD: *(to BENTLEY)* Say, uh, I don't suppose you could have a word to Simmo and ask him if he could perhaps . . . float me a bit of a loan, could you?

(Pause.)

BENTLEY: Would you like a beer?

RICHARD: Thanks.

(BENTLEY *goes out through the passageway.* SANDY *continues with her nails.* RICHARD *looks at her. Pause.)*

DIANE: Isn't this a beautiful place?

RICHARD: It certainly is.

SANDY: Yes, everyone raves about the unit.

RICHARD: So you're married to Bentley, eh?

SANDY: That's the present arrangement.

RICHARD: Funny to see old Bentley married. He was always a bit scared of girls. Never seemed to have the knack of cracking on. I remember he was wrapped in a bird called Doreen once, but he never made a move. Said he was biding his time, waiting for the right moment. But then Simmo got to her and it was too late. Old Bentley's got married, eh? I can hardly believe it.

SANDY: Neither can I.

RICHARD: Funny to see old Bentley married.

SANDY: What do you mean, 'funny'? What's so funny about it?

RICHARD: Well . . . it's . . . funny . . .

SANDY: Do you mean funny ha ha or funny peculiar? *(Pause.)*

RICHARD: Ha ha.

SANDY: Anyway, I won't be here for long. I'm on with Simmo now. We're going to make it together.

DIANE: I beg your pardon?

SANDY: I said Simmo and I are going to make it together.

DIANE: *(laughing)* Really, the fantasies some of these little hausfraus have!

SANDY: I'm Simmo's number one girl. We're going out this afternoon. He'll be here any minute.

DIANE: She must be dreaming. Simmo? Her? She's round the bend.

RICHARD: What's it to you, eh? What's it to you?

DIANE: Nothing.

RICHARD: *(to* SANDY*)* Could you sort of . . . put in a good word to Simmo about me?

(Pause. BENTLEY enters, carrying a tray on which there are four glasses of beer and a bottle.)

BENTLEY: Here we are. The old Resch's. Just like old times, eh Richard?

(BENTLEY hands the drinks around. DIANE sits down.)

RICHARD: Yeah.

BENTLEY: Well, chug-a-lug.

RICHARD: Chug-a-lug.

SANDY: Chug-a-lug.

(They look at her, hesitate, then drink.)

RICHARD: Been playing tennis, have you?

BENTLEY: Yeah. We won the doubles cup today. We were down two sets to love, then Gary got his big serve working, I chipped in at the net, and we were laughing. Towelled them up in no time.

SANDY: Congratulations.

(Pause. RICHARD looks around.)

RICHARD: Nice place you got here.

BENTLEY: Yes, it is rather. We've just moved in.

RICHARD: That's a very nice stereo set you've got there.

BENTLEY: A beauty, isn't it? Look what else I've got. *(He holds up the transistor radio.)*

RICHARD: What is it?

BENTLEY: A transistor radio, the latest model. Japanese.

RICHARD: Very compact, isn't it?

BENTLEY: Yes, it fits neatly into your pocket or purse. Pocket if you're a guy, and purse if you're a gal.

SANDY: Jesus.

(Pause.)

BENTLEY: Seen any of the old mob lately?

RICHARD: No, I seem to have lost touch.

BENTLEY: Yes, that tends to happen. You do lose touch.

RICHARD: Tell you what, I hear Hammo's back in town.

BENTLEY: Old chunder-guts, eh? He was a character, wasn't he?

RICHARD: A real character.

BENTLEY: We had some great times with old Hammo.

RICHARD: I'll say.

BENTLEY: Hey, do you remember the time he got pissed out of his mind and fronted up to this old duck and asked her for a root? It was Davo's mother! Jees I had to laugh. Nearly went off my face. Then the coppers came round and took him away. They put him in the paddy wagon with all the pros and cons. We had to go up to the cop shop and bail him out.

RICHARD: Bloody Hammo.

BENTLEY: He was a character, wasn't he?

RICHARD: A real character.

(The women are looking rather bored.)

BENTLEY: Remember the time he got sick at Davo's twenty-first and went for the big spit? He said to me, 'Jees I feel crook,' and then he raced across the room, shoved his head out the window and burped a rainbow.

It went all over Davo and his bird in the bushes. What a mess!

SANDY: Jees I had to laugh. Nearly went off my face.
(Pause.)

BENTLEY: I didn't know you knew Hammo.

SANDY: I don't.

BENTLEY: But how –

SANDY: Skip it.

(Pause.)

RICHARD: Those were the days.

BENTLEY: Remember the time . . .

(SANDY gets up and storms out of the room, through the passageway. BENTLEY watches her, then continues, glancing over his shoulder a couple of times.)

. . . when Hammo had a prang in his B and got dobbed in for neg driving?

RICHARD: Can't say I do.

BENTLEY: Well, Hammo had been on the grog and he didn't give way to his right and this bloke smashed into him. The bloke got all excited and was running all round the place like a mad thing, saying it was Hammo's fault. Well . . .

(SANDY enters, carrying a small step-ladder, which she places by the wall, L. They watch her. She goes out. BENTLEY continues uneasily.)

Well, Hammo wouldn't have a bar of that. 'My fault?' he said. 'That's a laugh. It's a wonder you haven't got a defect notice for that old bomb of yours.' Well, the bloke took exception to that, as you can well imagine. Then he tried to job Hammo. Well, Hammo got stuck into him, I can tell you. Laid him out like a used frog. But then the . . .

(SANDY enters, carrying a hammer, nail, and a picture, a vivid red abstract.)

Well, as I was saying, Hammo floored this twit, but then the coppers arrived and tried to pinch him . . .

(SANDY has climbed the ladder, and starts banging in the nail. BENTLEY tries to speak above the noise.)

. . . but Hammo said –

RICHARD: What?
BENTLEY: *(louder)* Hammo said –
RICHARD: I can't hear you!
BENTLEY: *(shouting)* SANDY!!
(SANDY *stops hammering.*)
SANDY: What?
BENTLEY: Uh, now darling, we have guests here and I'm finding it a little difficult trying to converse with them while you're making such a noise.
SANDY: Oh.
BENTLEY: So if you could just postpone your domestic activities until a more appropriate time, we would be very grateful.
SANDY: *(coming down the ladder)* Well now, how could I refuse a request like that.
BENTLEY: Thank you, darling. That's most considerate of you.
SANDY: Don't mention it, darling. I only want to please you.
(BENTLEY *smiles and turns to* RICHARD.)
BENTLEY: Isn't she a sweetie? A real darling. Don't you think I've made a good catch, eh Richard?
(BENTLEY *tries to put his arm around* SANDY.)
SANDY: Back.
(BENTLEY *retreats.*)
BENTLEY: Well, uh, as I was saying, the coppers threw the book at Hammo and they –
SANDY: Would you like another beer, Richard? I see you've finished.
RICHARD: Uh, yes, thank you.
(SANDY *gets the bottle.*)
BENTLEY: But Hammo said that no mug copper . . .
(SANDY *fills* RICHARD's *glass as* BENTLEY *speaks.*)
. . . is going to . . . push me around . . . but in the end they . . . pinched him. Anyway, that's what happened when Hammo had a prang in his B.
(SANDY *sits down.*)
RICHARD: Bloody Hammo.
(SANDY *looks up at* RICHARD.)

SANDY: What do you do?

RICHARD: What do you mean?

SANDY: What do you do? For a living. Do you make a living?

DIANE: Richard's the editor of *The Inevitable Tarantula*.

SANDY: What's *The Inevitable Tarantula*?

DIANE: You mean to say you've never heard of *The Inevitable Tarantula*?

SANDY: That's right. I've never heard of it.

DIANE: Well! Some people just don't know what's happening.

RICHARD: It's a sort of magazine. An underground magazine for artists.

BENTLEY: Richard was always the arty one at school. Did cartoons ... (SANDY *is looking at him*) ... humorous ...

SANDY: What else do you do?

RICHARD: I'm diversifying my activities in a number of different fields, like industrial design. I'm a painter mainly, but I do a few designs for the large glossies, too.

DIANE: You should have seen Richard's last one. It was a beaut design, a sort of tactile nightmare. He did this incredible white obelisk anchored into a beaut welter of blue streaks on a sheet of black strips with this incredible screen of pink flecks on a beaut steely surface.

SANDY: Sounds beaut.

DIANE: Richard's very clever, and he's got some very clever friends in the underground, too. It's marvellous fun. You meet all sorts of super people. Richard took me to a turn and I was really wrapped. There were all these incredibly tactile people throwing down Red Ned and saying such beaut things. Richard's got some fabulous friends. It's marvellous fun.

SANDY: Really?

DIANE: Richard's terribly clever. He's got tremendous artistic acumen and he's also abreast of the latest developments in industrial design.

BENTLEY: Yes, there has been a lot of astounding progress in industrial development in some of the many facets of modern technology.

(*Pause.* SANDY *stares at* BENTLEY *incredulously.*)

RICHARD: Bloody oath.

(RICHARD *sips his drink and looks at* SANDY.)

RICHARD: What do you do?

SANDY: Oh, lots of things. I'm always on the move, it's a mad whirl. I did a bit of modelling in Adelaide last year. And I'm thinking of doing a film in Melbourne in a month or two if I land a good role. I made a TV commercial here in Sydney not long ago.

RICHARD: What did you advertise?

SANDY: My legs.

(*Pause.*)

RICHARD: Oh.

(*He sips his drink.*)

SANDY: Panty-hose.

RICHARD: Oh, I see. That explains why . . . your legs . . .

SANDY: I found it a very absorbing experience.

RICHARD: Yes, I suppose it would be absorbing.

SANDY: I was absorbed, anyway.

RICHARD: What exactly did you have to do?

SANDY: Well, it started off with a B pulling up. It pulled up at the side of the street. I was driving it. I parked the car. Then the camera moved around and caught me getting out. I got out like this.

(*She moves her legs around to the side of the chair.*)

The camera was trained on my legs. I got out of the B.

(*She mimes it, and the rest of her speech.*)

I closed the door. Then I looked up and down the street. There was a man on the pavement.

(*She looks at* RICHARD.)

He looked at me. Then I went round to the parking metre. I stopped by the parking metre. The man was still watching me, but I didn't seem to mind. I gave the impression that I rather liked it. Then I slipped a coin in the slot of the metre. I walked across the pavement to a big glass building. I put my foot on the step like this. The camera was trained on my legs. The man's eyes followed me. I seemed to sense this, so I paused and looked around at him. He looked at me. Then I took a cigarette out of my bag and went up to him.

(She takes a cigarette out of her bag and goes up to RICHARD, holding the cigarette out.)

I asked him for a light.

(RICHARD fumbles in his pocket and brings out a cigarette lighter. He flicks it on and a great sheet of flame, about ten inches high, shoots up. He hastily flicks it off, smiles weakly at SANDY, and adjusts the dial on the lighter. He flicks it on. A small flame burns. SANDY lights her cigarette from the flame. She looks at RICHARD. She is standing very close to him.)

SANDY: Thank you.

(Pause.)

BENTLEY: Yes, and then what happened?

SANDY: *(impatiently)* Oh, then the jingle started – something about 'Sheer ecstasy in Ecstasy Sheers.'

BENTLEY: Oh I get it. Sheer in both senses. And ecstasy –

SANDY: Yes!

(She sits down. Pause.)

RICHARD: Do you like working in the pubic service, Bentley?

(Pause. RICHARD blushes slightly. BENTLEY considers the question.)

BENTLEY: I can't supply you with an unqualified categorical 'yes' or 'no' answer to that particular question. However, I should like to make it abundantly clear that I consider the position eminently suitable on a number of counts, but equally unsuitable on a number of other counts.

(Silence.)

SANDY: *(a soft wail)* Christ.

(Pause.)

DIANE: I've never seen her in a TV commercial.

RICHARD: Haven't you?

DIANE: No. I don't believe a word she says.

(The telephone rings. SANDY jumps up.)

SANDY: That'll be Simmo.

(She rushes over to the phone and picks up the receiver.)

Hello? Who? Oh, no! Look, I've had enough of you. Just stop bothering me, see? You what? You want to what? Good God! Look, if you don't stop all this I'll get Simmo on to you, see?

(She slams the receiver down.)

BENTLEY: Anyone we know?

SANDY: It was that dreadful Davo. Never gives up, the big oaf. I wish he'd stop bothering me.

BENTLEY: I'll have to speak to him.

(SANDY *stares at* BENTLEY.)

SANDY: You'll have to what?

BENTLEY: I'll have a quiet word with him. You know, intimate to him that you're not ... desirous ... to entertain his overtures.

SANDY: You mullet!

(She sits down.)

Do tell me a bit about yourself, Richard. What do you paint?

RICHARD: Pictures.

SANDY: I had already divined that. I mean, what sort? Abstract? Contemporary?

RICHARD: Well, contemporary, of course. I mean, we're all contemporary, aren't we? We're all alive.

SANDY: That's a moot point. Do you live at Paddington?

RICHARD: No.

SANDY: Oh. I would have thought you'd live at Paddington. And tell me, how long have you known the boy wonder?

RICHARD: Who?

SANDY: That. That over there. Whatsisname.

(BENTLEY *looks behind him.*)

RICHARD: That's Bentley. Your husband.

SANDY: I know.

RICHARD: You want to know how long I've known Bentley?

SANDY: Yes.

RICHARD: Oh. I didn't quite ... sort of ... understand ... to whom ... in effect ...

SANDY: Get on with it.

RICHARD: Yes well I've known Bentley since we were in kindergarten. We went through school, you see. We used to wag it together.

SANDY: Wag what?

RICHARD: Uh, school. Hookey, you know?

BENTLEY: Playing truant, I believe, is the correct expression for that particular misdemeanor.

SANDY: Thank you.

RICHARD: Well, anyway, Bentley and I lost touch after a while and this is the first time I've seen him for some years.

BENTLEY: Yes, it has been quite a while. You do lose touch.

RICHARD: How long have you two been married?

SANDY: A long, long time. I was quite young, what they call a slip of a girl, when Mr. Right turned up. That's him over there, in the neutral corner.

BENTLEY: I met Sandy at the local pictures one Saturday. It was a hot summer's night in the back stalls at the Roxy, and the organ was playing *Tea For Two*, and we were all eating Fantales and Sandy came in wearing a pink shift and I –

(A car horn is heard. SANDY jumps up.)

SANDY: At last! Simmo!

(She rushes over to the sideboard to get her handbag.)

Well, I'm off. Have yourselves a ball, peoples. There's a cold roast in the oven and a bottle of scotch in the cabinet so you should be set for the night. Ta-ta.

(Meanwhile, BENTLEY has taken something quietly from the cabinet drawer. He holds it behind his back.)

BENTLEY: Just a minute, Sandy.

(SANDY has her hand on the door knob. She turns and looks at him.)

I've got something for you.

(Pause.)

SANDY: What?
(Pause.)
BENTLEY: It's a surprise.
(Pause.)
SANDY: Well, what is it?
(Pause.)
BENTLEY: See if you can guess.
(Silence. BENTLEY produces a package wrapped in gaily-coloured paper.)
   Happy birthday, darling.
(Pause.)
   You thought I'd forgotten, didn't you?
(He advances towards her, singing.)
     Happy birthday to you
     Happy birthday to you
     Happy birthday, dear –
(He holds out the present to her. She knocks it to the floor, then goes out, slamming the door. BENTLEY looks at the closed door.)
     Happy . . . birthday . . . to . . .
(DIANE *gets up.*)
DIANE: Would you excuse me for a moment, please.
RICHARD: Where are you going?
DIANE: I just want to see Simmo. I won't be a minute.
RICHARD: But he's going out with Sandy. I mean, uh, apparently.
DIANE: I won't be a minute.
(DIANE *goes out the front door.*)
BENTLEY: Well, that's the little woman.
RICHARD: She's quite a girl.
BENTLEY: Ar, she's a good kid.
(Pause.)
   I love her very much.
(Pause.)
   I think there's something troubling her. She hasn't been very happy lately. It's been a big worry to me.
(Pause.)
   I'd like her to be happy.

(RICHARD *lights a cigarette.* BENTLEY *picks up the present and looks at it.*)

I bought her some panty-hose. Black mesh. They'll suit her.

(Pause.)

She's got lovely legs, don't you think?

(RICHARD *splutters on his cigarette.*)

RICHARD: Oh yes, lovely, lovely.

BENTLEY: She's a wonderful girl. I've always been very proud of her.

(He looks at the present.)

Black mesh.

RICHARD: I'm sure she'll like them.

(Pause.)

BENTLEY: Yes, I think there's something troubling her. I haven't heard her laugh for a long while. She used to be laughing all the time. Very gay. Always looked on the bright side of things. Very much alive. We used to go down to the beach. Park the B, dump the gear, and run into the surf, hand in hand. She'd hop about and shriek with joy. Pure joy. Like a child. Jumped up and down in the surf and splashed foam all over me. Not any more, though.

(He puts the present back in the drawer.)

Black mesh. I hope she likes them. She's a wonderful girl, don't you think?

RICHARD: Oh yes, wonderful. You're a very lucky man, Bentley.

BENTLEY: Yes, I've always been lucky.

(Pause.)

I won a chook at a pub once.

(Pause.)

Ay tell me, Richard, what exactly sort of made you come and see me after all this time?

(DIANE *comes in the front door.*)

RICHARD: What happened?

DIANE: Never mind.

BENTLEY: What made you come, Richard?

RICHARD: I wanted to see my old mate Bentley. I just thought we'd drop in, have a chat, sink a few . . . you know?

BENTLEY: Yeah?

RICHARD: Of course.

BENTLEY: Well, on behalf of my wife and I, I'd like to extend to you the very warmest of welcomes.

(Pause.)

RICHARD: Thank you. Nice place you got here.

BENTLEY: Yes, everyone raves about the unit.

RICHARD: I'm very impressed with your stereo set.

BENTLEY: Beauty, isn't it?

RICHARD: I'll say. What sort of records you got?

BENTLEY: We have a large and comprehensive selection of the best recordings in the popular, classical, and evergreen categories.

(Pause.)

RICHARD: Great.

BENTLEY: Look what else I've got. A tape recorder. Little beauty, isn't it?

RICHARD: Yeah.

BENTLEY: I'll show you how it works.

(BENTLEY switches on the machine, picks up the microphone and speaks into it.)
Testing 1-2-3.

(He reverses the tape to playback. SANDY's voice is heard on the tape.)

SANDY'S VOICE: I'm having it off with Simmo.

(BENTLEY's jaw drops. He turns off the tape recorder. He is very disconcerted. Silence.)

DIANE: I think we'd better be going.

RICHARD: Yes, we must be off.

BENTLEY: Sure you won't stay and have another beer?

RICHARD: No thanks.

BENTLEY: Would you prefer a scotch?

RICHARD: No thanks. I like scotch, but not after beer.

DIANE: I like gin and tonic, but not after rum and coke.

RICHARD: Vodka's not bad, but it hits you hard afterwards.

BENTLEY: You can't drink on an empty stomach.

RICHARD: Once you mix your drinks you've had it.

BENTLEY: Ever had a middy of Bacardi neat?

RICHARD: Bond Seven and water's good for a hangover.

BENTLEY: Those Bloody Marys pack a punch.

RICHARD: I like a highball for a nightcap.

BENTLEY: I'll never forget the first time I sank a screwdriver.

RICHARD: I like a scotch after a beer.

(Pause.)

DIANE: We really must be going.

RICHARD: You'll be all right, Bentley.

BENTLEY: Would you like to stay and hear a record?

RICHARD: No thanks, we've got to go.

BENTLEY: All right.

RICHARD: You'll be right, mate. Buck up.

BENTLEY: I'm all right.

RICHARD: Don't worry about it, mate. She'll come back to you.

DIANE: She won't last long with Simmo.

RICHARD: You'll win her back.

BENTLEY: You think so?

RICHARD: Of course. Just assert yourself a bit. Throw your weight around. Be more aggressive.

DIANE: Yes, don't take it lying down.

RICHARD: Pull your socks up and have a bash.

DIANE: You've got nothing to lose.

RICHARD: You'll soon be out of this bad patch you're going through, so cheer up. You may be down, but you're not out. I mean, after all, when you come down to it, your predicament isn't exactly one of cosmic proportions, now is it?

DIANE: You just tripped over and fell on the floor.

RICHARD: Chin up and toe the line, you'll soon be back on your feet.

BENTLEY: I'll do that.

RICHARD: Take designing, for instance. In designing, it's a question of putting things into context.

DIANE: It's the old relativity syndrome.

RICHARD: You've got to have a point of reference. It's the same with life.

DIANE: You've just got to have a point of reference.

RICHARD: It's as simple as that.

BENTLEY: I haven't got a point of reference.

RICHARD: Well, you see, then, that's where you're up yourself, isn't it? That's your trouble.

DIANE: You don't know whether you're slumming or growing.

RICHARD: You see, it's essential to have a framework to move in.

DIANE: Have you got a framework?

BENTLEY: No.

RICHARD: Well, that's your trouble, then, isn't it?

DIANE: You're between the deep blue sea and the frying pan.

RICHARD: You see, what you're lacking is an inner directive.

DIANE: You haven't got an inner directive.

RICHARD: That's your trouble.

DIANE: Too many put-on hang-ups, that's your problem.

RICHARD: What you really need is a meaningful stance.

BENTLEY: I haven't got a meaningful stance.

RICHARD: Well, you're buggered, then, aren't you? You've got to take action, get off your backside, move around. Think! Do! Be! Act!

(Pause.)

BENTLEY: Righto.

RICHARD: You've got no charisma.

DIANE: You've got a complex.

RICHARD: You need a rest.

DIANE: A complete break.

RICHARD: Rejuvenation.

DIANE: Regeneration.

RICHARD: Wake up to yourself.

DIANE: Wake up and live.

RICHARD: You'll be all right.

DIANE: You see what we mean?

BENTLEY: Yes.

RICHARD: Take the bull by the horns.

DIANE: Grab the nettle.

RICHARD: Face the facts.

DIANE: You'll be all right.

BENTLEY: Yes, I'll be all right. I'll take action.

RICHARD: That's the stuff. You'll win her back.

DIANE: Well, we'd better be going.

RICHARD: Yes, we really must fly. See you later, Bentley.

BENTLEY: Thanks for the advice.

DIANE: Think nothing of it.

RICHARD: It was a pleasure. After all, what are friends for?

DIANE: Goodbye.

BENTLEY: I could run you back in the B if you like.

RICHARD: No thanks, don't bother.

BENTLEY: Drop in any time. You know where we are.

RICHARD: Yes, it's a very easy place to find. You don't see many white hedges around these days.

BENTLEY: No, you don't.

RICHARD: Well, see you.

BENTLEY: Goodbye.

(RICHARD *opens the door.*)

  Oh, Richard.

RICHARD: What?

BENTLEY: Don't do anything I wouldn't do.

(Pause.)

RICHARD: Goodbye Bentley.

BENTLEY: Goodbye Richard.

(RICHARD *and* DIANE *exit.* BENTLEY *sits down and puts his hands to his face. Silence. The tape recorder suddenly crackles to life and* BENTLEY's *voice is heard on the tape.*)

BENTLEY'S VOICE: Testing 1-2-3.

(BENTLEY *picks up a cushion from the chair and hurls it at the tape recorder.*)

BLACKOUT

SCENE FOUR

Sunday afternoon, one week later. Lights up on SANDY *sitting in an armchair wearing a white dress. She is reading the Sunday paper and the audience can't see her face. Silence for a while, then* BENTLEY *enters, also dressed in white. He carries a quoit stand and five quoits. He places the quoit stand at the front of the stage and then steps back a few paces. He aims carefully, then throws the first quoit. It misses. He steadies himself and then throws the next four quoits very slowly, aiming carefully before each throw. They all miss and fall on the floor around the stand.* BENTLEY *stands very still and looks at the quoits on the floor. Then he looks at* SANDY, *who is still reading. Silence.* BENTLEY *goes over to the window and looks out of it. He lights a cigarette and gazes out of the window.* SANDY *continues reading.* BENTLEY *draws on his cigarette.*

CURTAIN

Act Two

SCENE ONE

The next day, Monday 6 p.m. Lights up on an empty stage. SANDY comes in through the passageway, carrying the step ladder and the red abstract. She hangs it on the wall and then takes the step ladder out through the passageway. She re-enters and goes into the bedroom. BENTLEY comes in the front door, wearing a suit and carrying a briefcase, a box of chocolates and a large bunch of flowers. He puts down the briefcase and holds the chocolates and flowers behind his back.

BENTLEY: Sandy? Where are you?
(Pause.)
   Sandy?
(SANDY comes out of the bedroom carrying a suitcase. She puts it down by the front door and goes back into the bedroom. She is wearing a black cocktail dress.)
   What's this? What are you doing with my suitcase?
(SANDY comes out of the bedroom carrying an airways bag.)
   What's the idea? What are you doing?
(SANDY puts the bag down by the front door and goes back into the bedroom. Small pieces of BENTLEY's gear – clothes, towels, tennis racquet, etc., are flung out through the bedroom door. BENTLEY goes over to the door.)
   I demand an explanation. I demand that you stop this immediately.
(BENTLEY ducks and a basketball bounces out over his head. SANDY comes out of the bedroom brushing her hair.)
SANDY: Simmo's moving in.
BENTLEY: What?
SANDY: You're moving out.
BENTLEY: Moving out? Moving out of my unit? You've got to be joking.
(Pause. SANDY continues brushing her hair.)
   You are joking, aren't you?

58

(Pause.)
In here? In my unit? I won't allow it.
(Pause.)
Look, uh, I bought you some chocolates and flowers,
darling.
(Pause.)
Maybe I haven't treated you too well lately, darling.
I don't know.
(Pause.)
Look, I tell you what. Let's go out to dinner tonight.
I'll give you the works – cocktails, dinner by candle-
light at a good restaurant, then a show, coffee at the
Cross, and home to bed. What do you say, huh?
SANDY: I'm going out to dinner with Simmo tonight.
BENTLEY: You could ring him up and say you've got
a headache. Tell him a little white lie. Say you've got
the pain you can't explain.
SANDY: You can move out now or you can sleep out
here tonight and find a flat tomorrow.
BENTLEY: That's ridiculous. I'm your husband.
SANDY: I know.
BENTLEY: You can't just throw me out.
SANDY: Why not?
(Pause.)
BENTLEY: Would you like to put these flowers in a
vase?
*(Pause. BENTLEY reaches into his briefcase and brings out a
copy of the Ladies'* Home Journal.*)*
I, uh, I've been doing a bit of reading, darling. I read
this article in the *Ladies' Home Journal* called 'Can This
Marriage Be Saved?' I think it's pretty relevant to
our problem, darling. Would you like to hear it?
(Pause. He reads:)
The trouble with Harry and Lottie's marriage was
that they didn't share each other's interests. So the
next vacation they sent Troy and Mary-Jane off to
summer camp and went fishing together at one of
Harry's favourite haunts.
(Pause.)

Would you like to come to the pub tomorrow night with me and Davo?

SANDY: You're moving out.

BENTLEY: What?

SANDY: Simmo's moving in.

BENTLEY: Over my dead body.

SANDY: If you insist.

(Pause.)

BENTLEY: You seem to have changed, darling. You seem all hard and cruel. You used to be a . . . terrific bird. I'd never have got to grade three if it hadn't been for you. Behind every successful man . . . you know? Alan White reckons I'm a moral for grade four, but I can't do it without you, darling.

(Pause.)

Remember the night we met? That night at the Roxy? I fell down the stairs and you said I was so helpless I needed someone to look after me. Do you remember that, darling?

SANDY: Stop it, Bentley.

BENTLEY: Look, why don't we just kiss and make up, eh?

SANDY: No.

BENTLEY: Would you like to open the chocolates?

SANDY: No.

BENTLEY: You're not being very co-operative, darling.

(Pause.)

You can't be serious. How can Simmo possibly move in here? This is my unit. That's my stereo set. You're my wife. You're my lawful wedded wife. You can't have Simmo in here. It's illegal. I can't envisage it. Simmo in my unit? It's out of the question. It's not on the board. You can't be serious.

SANDY: Look, what are you going to do? Simmo's moving in. What are you going to do?

BENTLEY: Simmo's not moving in here.

SANDY: He's moving in tonight.

BENTLEY: You're not having him here. Not in our home unit. I won't allow it.

SANDY: Won't you?

BENTLEY: No. I mean, I've got nothing against Simmo. I like the guy. I've found him to be an agreeable companion on a number of occasions. But he's shown a complete disregard for common courtesy.

SANDY: Has he?

BENTLEY: Yes. Look, if he's putting the hard word on you, if he's being in any way coercive, if he's employing intimidatory tactics of any kind, I'll take care of it. I'll have a man to man chat with him. Off the cuff, straight from the shoulder, no punches pulled. Everything open and above board. Clear the air, you know? Simmo's a good bloke, I'm open to reason, we'll work it out. We'll solve the problem. We'll nut it out together, me and Simmo. It'll be all taken care of.

SANDY: Je-sus.

BENTLEY: Well, what do you say?

SANDY: Simmo is moving in. You are moving out. Do I make myself clear?

(Pause.)

BENTLEY: Yes, darling, you have expressed your sentiments with force and clarity. However, the fact remains that Simmo is not moving in here. I don't like to be disagreeable, darling, but I feel that this proposal cannot be entertained under any circumstances. I'm sorry, but I can't allow him in here and that's that. Now if you would be so kind as to restore my personal effects to their proper place, I would be most grateful.

SANDY: Taking a firm stand, are you?

BENTLEY: You bet I am.

SANDY: Won't you relent?

BENTLEY: Certainly not.

SANDY: Pretty please?

BENTLEY: No.

SANDY: Well, I guess that's that, then.

BENTLEY: I'm putting my foot down.

SANDY: Please, oh please change your mind. Won't you relent? Won't you show us a little mercy? Where's your charity? Please let Simmo in. Please let him stay here. Please don't hurt him. I beg of you.

BENTLEY: *(beaten)* I'm ... taking a ... firm stand.

(A car horn is heard.)

SANDY: There's Simmo now.

(BENTLEY clears his throat hastily.)

BENTLEY: On the other hand, taking into account the extenuating circumstances motivating this plaintive request, I feel duty bound to reconsider the matter in the light of subsequent events.

SANDY: Thanks. You can sleep out here till you find a flat, if you like, or you can move out right now. Anyway, clean this place up. I'm going out to dinner with Simmo and when we come back I want this place to look clean.

(SANDY goes out the front door. BENTLEY stares after her. He looks around the room.)

FADE OUT

SCENE TWO

The following day, Tuesday, 6 p.m. BENTLEY sits in an armchair reading a newspaper. SANDY comes in wearing her black cocktail dress with lots of jewellery. She puts a tablecloth over the table and goes back out the passageway. She returns with expensive-looking china and cutlery and sets two places at the table. She puts out two wine glasses, an ice bucket with a bottle of champagne in it, and then brings out a candle-holder with one long candle in it. She lights the candle. During these preparations, BENTLEY keeps looking out from behind his newspaper. He tries to feign indifference. SANDY completes setting the table, and sits down in an armchair. She glances at her watch, brings out a small mirror from her handbag, and pats her hair into place. BENTLEY looks at her.

FADE OUT

SCENE THREE

The following day, Wednesday, 10 p.m. Lights up on an empty stage. SANDY can be heard giggling with pleasure from the bedroom, then silence. BENTLEY enters through the passageway, wearing pyjamas and bed socks and carrying a towel over his shoulder. He glances at the bedroom door, then gets into a makeshift bed, consisting of the two armchairs pushed together, with a rug over them. He reads the Ladies' Home Journal. *SANDY giggles again. BENTLEY looks at the bedroom door, then returns to his reading. SANDY starts giggling continuously. BENTLEY tries to continue reading, but then puts the magazine down in front of him. SANDY stops giggling. BENTLEY goes over to the wall and takes down the red abstract. He looks through a peephole into the bedroom. Silence. He wanders away, deep in thought, then goes out purposefully through the passageway and returns, carrying a hose, with his finger over the nozzle. He puts the hose through the peephole, and holds it there. Then, after a few moments, he withdraws it cautiously. There is no water coming out of the hose. He puts the hose back in the peephole, runs out through the passageway, and returns. He holds the hose, then cautiously withdraws it from the peephole. No water comes out of the hose. He runs out through the passageway, returns and holds the hose. He withdraws it cautiously. No water comes out of it. He peers up the nozzle. The hose squirts water in his face, then stops. He throws the hose on the floor. He strides out through the passageway and comes back with an air rifle. He marches up to the bedroom door, flings it open, stands back and aims the air rifle. He moves the barrel up and down, rhythmically. He is about to shoot when there is a knock on the door. BENTLEY hesitates, then lowers the rifle, closes the bedroom door, goes over and opens the front door. GARY and DIANE come in. GARY holds a large trophy. They both wear jeans and T-shirts depicting surfing scenes on the front.*

BENTLEY: Gary?
GARY: Bentley.
BENTLEY: Gary.
GARY: Bentley.
BENTLEY: Hello Gary.
GARY: Hello Bentley.
(Pause.)
  You know Diane, don't you?
BENTLEY: Hello Diane.
DIANE: Hello Bentley.
(Pause.)
BENTLEY: Well, good to see you.
GARY: Yeah. We just dropped in. Nothing special.
DIANE: We just dropped in.
BENTLEY: What have you been up to?
GARY: Nothing much. What about you?
BENTLEY: Ar, just mucking around as usual. *Comme ci, comme ça.* Been down the rubbity lately?
GARY: No, I haven't hit the hops for a couple of weeks. Why?

BENTLEY: Nothing. You haven't heard anything about me, have you? Any sort of . . . rumours, have you?

GARY: Rumours?

BENTLEY: Yes.

GARY: No.

BENTLEY: That's good. You know how these things get around . . . give a false impression . . . just a pack of lies.

GARY: What sort of rumours?

BENTLEY: Oh, you know the kind of thing . . . absolute rubbish. Smoke with no fire. So you haven't heard anything?

GARY: Not a word.

BENTLEY: That's great.

GARY: How's Sandy?

BENTLEY: Fine, just fine.

GARY: That's great. How's the world been treating you?

BENTLEY: No worries.

GARY: Glad to hear it.

BENTLEY: Well, how about a beer?

GARY: Wouldn't say no.

BENTLEY: Won't be a minute.

(BENTLEY *goes out through the passageway.*)

DIANE: Well, where is he?

GARY: Probably in the bedroom.

DIANE: With her?

GARY: Probably.

DIANE: What could he want with her?

GARY: A game of bridge, probably.

DIANE: I don't understand it. She's a nothing.

GARY: Look, what's it to you?

DIANE: Nothing.

GARY: Eh?

DIANE: Forget it.

GARY: You couldn't possibly be aspiring to Simmo's cot, now could you?

DIANE: Of course I'm not. What a suggestion!

GARY: It's just as well.

DIANE: Why?

GARY: I've seen it happen time and again. You stick with me.

DIANE: Of course I'll stick with you. What do you think I am?

(Pause.)

Of course I'll stick with you.

(BENTLEY *re-enters with three beers.*)

BENTLEY: Here we are. The old Resch's.

GARY: Thanks, mate.

BENTLEY: Chug-a-lug.

GARY: Chug-a-lug.

DIANE: Cheers. *(They drink.)*

BENTLEY: Just dropped in, have you?

GARY: Yes, we were passing by and we thought we might pop in and see our old mate Bentley.

DIANE: We saw Simmo's B outside.

BENTLEY: Oh?

DIANE: Yes. We thought we might pop in and see our old friend Simmo.

BENTLEY: Did you?

DIANE: Yes. Gary wants a job in Simmo's firm.

BENTLEY: What firm?

GARY: Simmo Enterprises Ltd.

BENTLEY: I'm sorry to disappoint you, but Simmo's not here.

DIANE: But we saw his B outside.

BENTLEY: You must have been mistaken.

DIANE: You can't mistake Simmo's B.

BENTLEY: The Prime Minister's got a flat on the ground floor. Maybe Simmo's visiting the Prime Minister.

(Pause.)

GARY: Where's Sandy?

BENTLEY: She's in bed. She was very tired.

(Pause.)

GARY: Nice place you've got here. Must be handy to the beach.

BENTLEY: Yes, hop in the B, you're there in a tick.

(GARY *picks up* BENTLEY's *air rifle.*)

GARY: Say, is this your old air rifle?

BENTLEY: That's the one.

GARY: I remember you had this at school.

BENTLEY: Yeah. Remember the time we got every street light along the beach that night?

GARY: Do I ever! Remember that old duck who chased us up the promenade?

BENTLEY: She had Buckley's. Remember the time when Hammo knocked off the light in front of the cop shop?

GARY: Bloody Hammo. Hey, remember the time when you shot Simmo in the arse in the playground at school?

BENTLEY: Yes.

GARY: Hey, look, there's still a dent in the barrel where Simmo hit you on the head.

(Pause.)

BENTLEY: *(to* DIANE) Can I top up your glass?

DIANE: No thanks.

GARY: Reminds me of the time when Hammo told Simmo he didn't like the way Simmo was running the playground. Poor Hammo. He was in a coma for three days. Still, he was the only bloke who ever stood up to Simmo.

(Pause.)

BENTLEY: What's the trophy for?

DIANE: Gary won the Senior Surf Race at the Manly Surf Carnival.

BENTLEY: Congratulations.

DIANE: Isn't he marvellous?

GARY: Ar jees.

DIANE: We're going on a surfari next week. We're going up the coast in Gary's B. I love surfing. Gary lent me his board one day and I was really wrapped. It's the only thing worth doing. We're going to take three weeks off and follow the sun.

BENTLEY: Great.

DIANE: Gary's managed to successfully bridge the gap between the surf clubs and the board riders. He's both a club member and a board rider. He's been the first to bridge this great chasm.

(DIANE *puts the trophy down on the sideboard beside* BENTLEY's *much smaller tennis trophy.*)

BENTLEY: It's a very handsome trophy.

GARY: Thanks.

DIANE: We're going to show it to Simmo.

BENTLEY: Why?

DIANE: It's Gary's reference. Simmo's bound to ask Gary to join his firm when he sees the trophy.

BENTLEY: What sort of firm is this Simmo Enterprises Ltd?

GARY: Well, it's sort of hard to explain, Bentley.

DIANE: It's very exciting.

BENTLEY: I see.

(SANDY *giggles from the bedroom.*)

GARY: What was that?

BENTLEY: What?

GARY: That noise.

BENTLEY: I didn't hear anyone giggling.

GARY: Maybe I was mistaken.

DIANE: Well, I think we'd better be going.

GARY: Sure you haven't seen Simmo?

BENTLEY: Positive.

DIANE: You don't know where we could find him?

BENTLEY: No idea. Try the pub.

GARY: Righto. Well, see you, Bentley.

BENTLEY: See you.

GARY: If you do happen to bump into Simmo, then –

(SANDY *whirls out of the bedroom, wearing a short flimsy nightdress with a see-through top.*)

SANDY: Simmo wants a cigarette. Are there any cigarettes?

(Pause.)

I said Simmo wants a cigarette.

(Pause.)

What are you doing here?

GARY: We just dropped in.

DIANE: We were just passing by and we dropped in.

SANDY: Oh. Have you got any cigarettes? Simmo
   wants a cigarette.

GARY: Here you are.

(GARY *hands her a packet of cigarettes.*)

SANDY: Thank you.

GARY: Give my regards to Simmo.

(DIANE *walks over to the bedroom door.*)

SANDY: What do you think you're doing?

DIANE: Just having a look.

SANDY: How dare you snoop around in my unit!

GARY: Come on, Diane. Cut it out.

(DIANE *goes over to the armchair and sits down, guided by*
GARY.)

SANDY: What's the matter with you? Is that how you
   get your kicks? Are you a voyeur? We've already had
   one voyeur this evening. A Peeping Tom. Looking at
   us. Getting an eyeful. How do you think we feel? Uh?

GARY: She's sorry.

SANDY: I mean, I'm liberal-minded, but I draw the
   line at voyeurs. So does Simmo. He'll take action if
   there's any more.

GARY: There won't be any more. Tell Simmo I've put
   a stop to it.

SANDY: I should think so. We don't like it. I mean,
   we've already got a resident Peeping Tom as it is. A
   full-time voyeur. We don't want any more. One's
   more than enough. Anyway, we're getting rid of him.
   He's going to leave. Isn't he?

(Pause.)

   Isn't he?

(Pause.)

   Yes, we're getting rid of him. I mean, it's a bit much,
   isn't it? Simmo finds it very tiresome. What do you
   suggest we do?

GARY: I'm . . . not sure.

BENTLEY: Would anyone like another beer?

(Pause.)

SANDY: Bentley is a public servant. He's a very good public servant. They think very highly of him in the department. I'm very proud of Bentley. Very proud. I gave him five years of my nubile period. Five years.

BENTLEY: Five and a half.

SANDY: Five and a half. But all good things must come to an end, don't you feel? You can have too much of a good thing, don't you agree?

GARY: I'm . . . not sure.

SANDY: You're not sure? I think it's very clear-cut. It's as plain as the nose on your little friend's face. It's crystal clear. There's only one course of action, don't you think? Uh?

GARY: I'm not . . . certain.

SANDY: Well I am. I'm certain. Thanks for the cigarettes.

(She goes back into the bedroom. Silence.)

BENTLEY: That's a very nice trophy you've got there, Gary.

GARY: You like it?

BENTLEY: Very much.

GARY: Thanks.

DIANE: Nice place you've got here.

BENTLEY: You like it?

DIANE: Very much.

BENTLEY: Thanks.

(Pause. GARY gets up. So does DIANE.)

GARY: I think we'd better be going.

DIANE: It's getting late.

BENTLEY: Yes.

GARY: Thanks for the grog.

BENTLEY: My pleasure.

(Pause.)

GARY: Don't worry about it too much, Bentley. You'll be all right.

DIANE: Yes, don't let her upset you.

GARY: Just ignore her.

BENTLEY: I'll do that.

DIANE: Don't take any notice of her.

BENTLEY: I don't.

GARY: What you should do is get out and about more.

DIANE: There are plenty of other fish in the sea.

GARY: Find yourself another bird.

DIANE: That'll make her jealous.

GARY: Don't let it get you down.

DIANE: Live it up.

GARY: Have a bash.

DIANE: Take a chance.

GARY: Play it cool.

DIANE: What can you lose?

GARY: You'll be home and hosed in no time.

BENTLEY: You reckon?

GARY: Look, why don't you come down to the pub tomorrow night? Have a few beers, forget your worries. You might bump into Hammo down there.

BENTLEY: Hammo?

GARY: Yes, I hear he's back in town.

BENTLEY: Old Hammo, eh? I hope he makes it.

GARY: I'll line up a bird for you, too. I know a couple of grunters.

DIANE: You'll be all right.

GARY: What do you say?

BENTLEY: I'll see you tomorrow.

GARY: Great. Well, we'll be off.

DIANE: Goodbye.

GARY: Find your feet, get your head down, keep your eye on the ball.

DIANE: Keep your eyes peeled and your nose clean.

GARY: You've got to get your foot in the door before you throw your weight around. That's the first step. The second step is to put your best foot forward. And step number three is to keep on your toes. Follow me?

BENTLEY: Yes.

DIANE: Don't worry about it. Simmo won't be here for long.

GARY: See you tomorrow.

BENTLEY: Hoo roo.

GARY: Oh, by the way. Here are the photos from your house-warming party.

(GARY *hands some photos to* BENTLEY. BENTLEY *looks at them.*)

BENTLEY: Thanks.

GARY: There's a good snap of you and Sandy by the stereo set.

BENTLEY: Beauty.

GARY: See you.

(GARY *and* DIANE *go out the front door.* BENTLEY *sits down and puts his hands to his face. Then he turns off the top light and reads in bed by the light of the lamp.* SANDY *comes quietly out of the bedroom. She looks at him.*)

SANDY: Are you awake, Bentley?

BENTLEY: Yes.

SANDY: What are you reading?

BENTLEY: The *Ladies' Home Journal.*

SANDY: Is it interesting?

BENTLEY: Oh yes. I'm reading about how Chuck and Betty's marriage was on the rocks because of in-law trouble.

SANDY: That's nice. Are you comfortable there?

BENTLEY: Oh yes. I was a bit stiff after the first night, but I put a cushion in the crook of my back and slept like a log.

SANDY: That's good. It must be a bit awkward, having to sleep out here.

BENTLEY: Well, like everything else, it has its virtues and its defects, but in the long run, taking into account all the relevant factors, the defects outweigh the virtues.

SANDY: Yes, I suppose they would.

BENTLEY: This doesn't mean that the virtues are non-existent. Far from it. It's just that they are disproportionate to the defects.

(BENTLEY *puts his fist into his mouth and bites it hard.*)

SANDY: Of course. Now, Bentley, Simmo and I have just had a small conference, and he was all for . . . causing you bodily harm. He was going to inflict bodily pain on you. He felt that it was a necessary step to take, and one which was essential to his personal well-being. But I prevented him. I said: 'Bentley will go. You leave it to me.' So there you have it. Either you go, or . . . well . . .

BENTLEY: I don't see why I should go.

SANDY: You don't?

BENTLEY: No. It's my unit. I live here.

SANDY: I see.

BENTLEY: A man's home is his castle.

SANDY: Go on.

BENTLEY: That's a review of the current situation, from my point of view.

SANDY: That's your considered opinion, is it?

BENTLEY: Yes.

(Pause.)

SANDY: I think I've been very patient. I've been able to retain my cool. But really, I do think that you're taking me within sight of breaking point. I'm in control, I've maintained my equanimity, but I'm on the brink, do you understand? Are you going to play ball? Are you going to get out? Or is Simmo going to have to break your skull?

BENTLEY: I don't feel we've considered all the available alternatives.

SANDY: You see this air rifle? Would you like Simmo to wrap it round your head?

(Pause.)

Look, Simmo can't stand it any longer. There's been talk down at the pub. Adverse comment. He's had to thump three blokes in the last week. They were making jokes. How do you think I feel? I'll be a laughing stock if this keeps up. You'll have to go. There's no alternative. If you're not out by the end of the week, then . . . *(shrugging)* huh . . .

BENTLEY: I'll consider your request.

SANDY: Look, Benny . . .

(Pause. They look at each other.)

Look, I don't want to see you get hurt. So just move out, will you?

(Pause.)

It's finished, Bentley. It's all over.

BENTLEY: Is it?

SANDY: Yes.

BENTLEY: I'm sorry, but I've worked very hard for this unit, and I'm the legal tenant of the premises, and I will not be forced out of my unit. I will not give up the ship. Anyone desirous of buying my property will have to submit their proposal through the proper channels.

SANDY: You'll be sorry.

(SANDY goes back into the bedroom. BENTLEY lights a cigarette and smokes nervously. He goes to the telephone, dials a number, and waits.)

BENTLEY: Hello? Could I speak to your sergeant, please constable? Yes, maybe you could. I have a complaint to make. Is it strictly legal for a bloke to break into another bloke's unit and kick out the bloke who owns the unit? That's what I thought. Yes, it's happened to me. Would you? Great. I'll see you in five minutes. Oh, uh, Simmo. Hello? Hello? Hello?

(He hangs up. Then he dials another number.)

Hello? Sorry to disturb you at this hour, Mr. Shapiro, but I've got a very urgent legal problem on my hands. Well, a bloke's moved into my unit and now he's going to kick me out. Yes. That's what I reckon. Good. Well, uh, Simmo. What do you mean, I haven't got a leg to stand on legally? Hello? Hello? Hello?

(BENTLEY hangs up and goes back to bed. He stares in front of him, then picks up his magazine and reads. SANDY giggles from the bedroom. BENTLEY puts down the magazine and stares in front of him. SANDY giggles again.)

FADE OUT

SCENE FOUR

The following evening, 6 p.m. Lights up on an empty stage. BENTLEY *enters through the passageway, wearing jeans and a T-shirt. He picks up his suitcase and puts it by the front door. He switches on the tape recorder, picks up the microphone, and speaks into it.*

BENTLEY: Dear Sandy. This is your husband Bentley speaking. In view of recent events, and taking all the various factors appertaining to the situation into consideration, I wish to inform you that I am leaving you for a period of trial separation. Being married to you, while enjoyable in many aspects, has placed severe limitations on my freedom of movement, as I have what may be termed a roving eye, and wish to indulge my inclinations in that field of endeavour. I have decided to seek greater freedom and greener pastures and will embark on a new way of life. As I set out to seek my fortune, I leave you with a thought for today which I hope will console you: It is better to have loved and lost than never to have loved at all, so don't feel too badly about it. The same thing happened to Chuck and Betty when their marriage went on the rocks. So there it is. I'll say goodbye now, and embark on my new way of life, freed from all shackles, and eager to embrace new experiences. I don't wanna break your heart, woman, but hell, I gotta keep a-travellin' on. So it's time to say goodbye, I guess. This is your husband Bentley signing off. Goodnight and God bless.

(He switches off the machine, looking very pleased with himself. Then he switches to playback. SANDY's *voice is heard on the tape.)*

SANDY'S VOICE: Piss off.

BLACKOUT

CURTAIN

Act Three

SCENE ONE

The following Saturday morning. The curtain rises on another curtain, a black one, a few feet behind it. Dangling on a string from the ceiling is a meat pie. It is about six feet off the floor. Silence for a while, then RICHARD and GARY enter from opposite sides and walk up to the pie. They look at it. GARY carries a rifle. They look at the pie. Silence.

GARY: Is this it?
RICHARD: That's it.
GARY: Is this all?
RICHARD: Yes.
(Pause.)
GARY: Very effective.
RICHARD: You like it?
GARY: Very much.
RICHARD: Thanks.
GARY: It's a beauty.
RICHARD: I'm happy with it.
GARY: What's it called?
RICHARD: 'Still Life'.
GARY: Very appropriate.
RICHARD: You think so?
GARY: Very much so.
RICHARD: Thanks.
GARY: It's well named.
RICHARD: I'm glad to hear it.
(GARY pushes the pie. It swings to and fro like a pendulum.)
GARY: What do you call it now?
RICHARD: 'Pie in the Sky'.
GARY: Very apt.
RICHARD: Do you think so?
GARY: I do indeed.

75

RICHARD: Thanks.

(Pause. GARY looks around.)

GARY: Bit stuffy in here.

(RICHARD stops the pie swinging, then goes to the side of the stage and pulls the black curtain back, revealing the rest of the room.)

That's better.

RICHARD: I always like to keep the still lifes separated when they're being shown for the first time.

GARY: Good idea.

(They walk back into the main part of RICHARD's room. It is designed the same way as BENTLEY's living room, with a door, down R., a passageway up L., and a window in the right wall, upstage. The walls are brown. There are paintings everywhere and a junk sculpture in a prominent position. It consists of an old cash register with two giant pink plastic handles, mounted on a stand. There is a bed, bookcase, chairs, tables, record-player, and a curved Japanese sword mounted on the back hall.)

Mum tells me you're leaving us.

(RICHARD starts packing a suitcase and tidying up the room.)

RICHARD: That's right. I've decided to go bush and sort myself out.

GARY: What happened to that magazine you edited?

RICHARD: Unfortunately *The Inevitable Tarantula* is now defunct. I tried to borrow some money to keep it afloat, but I failed. Then all my staff walked out on me, including my old friend Diane.

GARY: She's a tart, that one.

RICHARD: She's a whore.

GARY: Well, she's finally got what she wants.

RICHARD: Yes. So there you are. I dropped the lot. I battled away on the outer for years. but where did it get me? I'm going bush, mate. They can all get stuffed.

GARY: Anyway, Richard, we'll be sorry to lose you. You've been a model tenant.

RICHARD: I do my best.

GARY: Bet you'll miss Mum's cooking.

RICHARD: Yes.

GARY: No more rissoles for breakfast.

RICHARD: No.

GARY: Well, I suppose I'd better be off.

RICHARD: Going hunting, are you?

GARY: Yeah, going up to Werris Creek for the weekend.

RICHARD: Who with?

GARY: Simmo, of course. He'll be round any minute to pick me up in the B. He knows all the best places to go.

RICHARD: Well, have a good time.

GARY: We will, mate, don't worry. We always do. Gaw, I remember the last time we went up the country with Simmo. Did I ever tell you about it? We had a great time. We blew into this little hick town on a Saturday morning and by midnight that night do you know what Simmo had done?

RICHARD: No, Gary, do tell me.

GARY: He backed five winners at the picnic races, floored three locals in a brawl, demolished a niner, and torpedoed the minister's daughter. Anglican, she was. High Church.

RICHARD: Bloody Simmo, eh?

GARY: I bet they're still talking about it. But you wait till we hit Werris Creek tonight, mate, it'll be even wilder. Gaw, I remember the last time we were there. We had a great time that day. I was in the pub having a quiet beer with a few Werris Creek identities, when this bloke came up and started picking a blue with Simmo. Christ! It was suicide! Well, anyway, he copped the lot from Simmo, as you can well imagine. I couldn't bear to watch it, so I ducked out for a Johnny Bliss. But when I came back it was a real donnybrook – Simmo took on the lot of them and came out without a scratch.

RICHARD: That's Simmo for you.

GARY: Bloody oath. What a man!

RICHARD: What a man.

GARY: Anyway, Richard, I'll be off now. All the best.

RICHARD: Same to you.

GARY: Keep on with your art, mate. You'll crack it one day, I'm sure of it. I mean, you're nobody's fool, mate. You've got a bit of nouse.

RICHARD: Thanks, Gary.

GARY: I mean, you might be an arty sort of bloke, but you've got your head screwed on the right way. You don't bung on the bull like a lot of these blokes you see around the place these days. Now take these pictures, for instance. Now I wouldn't pretend to know what they're all about, because maybe I'm not too cluey about this sort of thing. But I do know this: you're not bunging on the bull, mate.

RICHARD: Thanks, Gary, I try to keep it clean. As a matter of fact, I remember when I had my one and only exhibition at an art gallery, there was a whole lot of scientists there, bunging it on. They were on a lunch-break from a convention on dynamics and they said my work was symptomatic.

GARY: Symptomatic, eh?

RICHARD: Yes.

GARY: They were having you on.

RICHARD: That occurred to me, Gary.

GARY: What a lot of bull-artists. Bloody scientists. What were they doing in an art gallery, anyway? But you're not like that, Richard. You're a good bloke. You play it straight.

RICHARD: Thank you, Gary.

GARY: Well, I must say it's been a pleasure having you here, Richard. You've done the right thing by me and I'd say I've done the right thing by you, and you can't do better than that. I mean, if a bloke, no matter who he is, does the right thing by a bloke, and that bloke does the right thing by the other bloke, then you can't go fairer than that, now can you?

RICHARD: I don't think so.

GARY: Anyway, take care of yourself, don't get on the hops too much, keep your nose clean and your feet dry and you can't go wrong.

RICHARD: I'll do that, Gary.
GARY: All the best, mate.
RICHARD: Same to you.
GARY: Drop us a line.
RICHARD: Will do.
GARY: Take care.
RICHARD: Keep in touch.
GARY: Will do.
(There is a knock on the door.)
RICHARD: Come in.
(BENTLEY *enters timidly. He wears jeans and a T-shirt and carries a suitcase.)*
  Bentley?
BENTLEY: Gary?
RICHARD: Hello Bentley.
BENTLEY: Hello Richard, Gary.
GARY: Bentley.
(Pause.)
RICHARD: Well, this is a surprise.
BENTLEY: Yes.
GARY: What brings you here, Bentley?
BENTLEY: I just thought I'd drop in on my old mates.
RICHARD: Good to see you.
BENTLEY: I don't suppose you've seen Hammo around, have you?
RICHARD: Not recently.
GARY: I hear he's back in town.
BENTLEY: Good. I hope I can find him.
(GARY *looks at his watch and goes to the window.)*
GARY: Simmo should be here any minute.
BENTLEY: Who?
GARY: Simmo.
BENTLEY: Oh.
RICHARD: Gary's going shooting with Simmo.
BENTLEY: That's nice.
GARY: How are things with you, Bentley?
BENTLEY: Fine. Just fine.
RICHARD: How's the old public service?
BENTLEY: I don't know. I tossed it in.

GARY: What?

RICHARD: Well, who'd have thought!

BENTLEY: Yeah, does seem a bit strange. No more super.

GARY: Why'd you leave?

(BENTLEY *clears his throat.*)

BENTLEY: I decided I needed to undergo some re-orientation of the underlying factors governing my basic attitudes to life, liberty, and the pursuit of happiness.

(*Pause.*)

RICHARD: Good idea.

BENTLEY: Anyway, I was about to get the boot from work, so I decided to resign. Simmo rang up my department. Had a word to Alan White and out I went.

GARY: Bad luck.

BENTLEY: Not really. I was sick of the place. I was in a rut, you see. I felt that life has more to offer.

RICHARD: You reckon?

GARY: (*looking out the window*) Here's Simmo now.

(*A car horn is heard. BENTLEY dives under RICHARD's bed.*)

What on earth . . . ?

RICHARD: Hey Bentley! What's going on?

GARY: It was only a car horn.

RICHARD: What's the matter, Bentley? Come out of there. What are you scared of?

GARY: Maybe he's scared of Simmo.

BENTLEY: Scared of Simmo? That's a laugh. Ha!

RICHARD: Come out from under that bed. You're making a fool of yourself.

BENTLEY: Who says I'm scared of Simmo? I could take him any day.

GARY: Now I've heard everything. Well, I'll be off now. See you, Bentley. All the best, Richard.

(*They shake hands.*)

RICHARD: Look after yourself.

GARY: Don't forget to write.

RICHARD: Give my regards to Simmo.

GARY: Righto. See you, mate.

(GARY *goes out.*)

RICHARD: All right, Bentley, now what's the idea?

BENTLEY: Is he gone?

RICHARD: Who?

BENTLEY: Simmo.

(RICHARD *goes over to the window.*)

RICHARD: Yes, there goes the B now.

(BENTLEY *crawls out from under the bed, looking around cautiously.*)

BENTLEY: I wasn't all that keen to see Simmo.

RICHARD: Oh.

(BENTLEY *indicates* RICHARD's *suitcase.*)

BENTLEY: Going somewhere?

RICHARD: Yes, I'm going bush to sort myself out.

BENTLEY: Good idea.

RICHARD: Tell me, how's your lovely wife?

BENTLEY: I don't know. She's living with Simmo in our home unit.

RICHARD: Bad luck.

BENTLEY: Yes, it is, rather.

RICHARD: Well, it's great to see you. Funny you should turn up here.

BENTLEY: Well, I wasn't going anywhere in particular, so I thought I might drop in.

RICHARD: Well, uh, like a beer?

BENTLEY: Thanks.

(RICHARD *goes out through the passageway.* BENTLEY *looks apprehensively around him. He sees the dangling pie, goes over and looks at it.* RICHARD *enters with two glasses of beer.*)

RICHARD: Here we are. The old Resch's. Down the hatch.

BENTLEY: Chug-a-lug.

(*They drink.*)

RICHARD: Living with Simmo, is she?

BENTLEY: Yes.

RICHARD: I'm sorry to hear that. Must be a bit of a blow.

BENTLEY: Yes. Well, no, actually, not really.

RICHARD: What do you mean?

BENTLEY: I could see it coming. She only did it to spite me, you know.

RICHARD: Oh?

BENTLEY: Yeah, she heard all about my . . . exploits, and so she just did it out of spite.

RICHARD: What exploits?

BENTLEY: Well, you know, the usual thing, having a bit on the side. I mean, we're both men of the world, aren't we? You know what I'm talking about, don't you?

RICHARD: I think so.

BENTLEY: We finally had a showdown when she caught me in flaggers with a bit of fluff. 'All right, you stupid bitch,' I said, 'run off with Simmo and see where it gets you. Me, I'm on clover – been fighting them off with a stick. Don't you worry about me, sweetheart.' She was madly jealous, you see. It had to end this way. 'All right,' I said, 'off you go. A clean break. No hard words. Okay with me. Anyway, it'll give me a free hand – that's one good thing. But,' I said to her, 'don't come crawling to me when Simmo gives you the boot. You just keep out of my sight. I'll be busy living it up in the cot and I won't want you mucking things around. And furthermore,' I said, really giving it to her, 'and furthermore – '

(*He leans on the cash register sculpture while making his point. It rings and the cash drawer pops out.* BENTLEY *stumbles, nearly falls over, then retreats a few paces, gaping at the machine.*)

What's that?

RICHARD: A sculpture.

BENTLEY: What's it called?

RICHARD: 'Cash and Carry'.

BENTLEY: I see. Yes, it's very effective. Always the arty one, weren't you?

(He looks around the room.)

RICHARD: Huh. I suppose so.

BENTLEY: Nice room you got here.

RICHARD: Like it?

BENTLEY: Yes, it's very well appointed. *(Indicating the pie)* That's an interesting piece of work.

RICHARD: Yes, it's from my brown period. I'm quite fond of it. It has a symphonic density which I find rather appealing.

BENTLEY: It's not bad, but I think it needs a bit of oomph.

(Pause.)

RICHARD: A bit of what?

(Pause.)

BENTLEY: Oomph.

(Pause.)

RICHARD: I'm afraid I haven't got any oomph.

BENTLEY: I remember at school you were always the arty one. Always sketching the teachers. Everyone said you had a brilliant future. And cartoons, too. I remember those cartoons you used to draw. Huh. Bloody funny, some of them. I can still see that one of Davo. Sent him up sky high. Remember it?

RICHARD: Vaguely.

BENTLEY: What a laugh! You did a cartoon of Simmo once, didn't you?

RICHARD: Yes.

BENTLEY: What happened to it?

RICHARD: Simmo tore it up.

BENTLEY: Why?

RICHARD: He said it wasn't in the public interest.

BENTLEY: Bloody Simmo, eh? Done any more cartooning?

RICHARD: No, not for a long while.

BENTLEY: That's a pity.

RICHARD: I've been going on too many benders lately.

BENTLEY: Benders?

RICHARD: Yes, I sort of leave home, get out on the grog, sleep in the park, and ... have a ball. Gary found me in the gutter outside the pub and said I could stay here in the spare room for a while.

BENTLEY: You don't suppose that ... well, now that you're going ...

RICHARD: I'm sure Gary'll put you up.

BENTLEY: It's just temporary, you realise. Till I get back on my feet. I've got to find a point of reference.

RICHARD: Of course.

BENTLEY: I knew I could count on my old mates. That's why I came here. I'm going to look around, find Hammo, size up the prospects. I've got a lot of faith in my old mates.

RICHARD: We all used to be great mates, didn't we?

BENTLEY: I'll say. Huh. Times we used to have!

RICHARD: Thick as thieves, weren't we?

BENTLEY: That's for sure. Do you still remember what we used to get up to at school?

RICHARD: Do I ever!

BENTLEY: Hey, remember that last football match, the grand final when Davo got barrelled?

RICHARD: What match was that?

BENTLEY: You remember, the one against Tykeland. I heard one of them say, 'Get the big bloke!' and when the ruck broke up, Davo was flat on his back and out like a light. Little red-headed Tyke got him.

RICHARD: Can't recall that occasion.

BENTLEY: But Simmo got even. Behind the ref's back. That little red-headed Tyke never got up.

RICHARD: I don't remember that.

(Pause.)

BENTLEY: But you were there. You helped carry him off.

RICHARD: Huh. Must have forgotten.

(Pause.)

Old Davo. What a funny bloke. Remember the time when Hammo had a copy of *Lady Chat* in his locker and we all looked at it one lunchtime?

BENTLEY: No, what happened?

RICHARD: Well, it was too much for old Davo when he saw the dirtiest bit, on page fifty-five.

BENTLEY: I thought the dirtiest bit in *Lady Chat* was on page thirty-four.

RICHARD: Oh. Could be. Well, anyway, it was too much for old Davo. He crept off to the bog and got a grip on himself.

BENTLEY: I don't recall that.

(Pause.)

RICHARD: But you were there. You read it out to him. I can still see you, standing in front of the Honour Roll.

BENTLEY: Huh. Must have slipped my mind. I remember when Hammo had a copy of *The Sex Life of Robinson Crusoe*.

RICHARD: No, it was *Lady Chat*.

BENTLEY: Funny, I must have forgotten all about it.

(Pause.)

Hey, I tell you what I do remember, the night Susan went off.

RICHARD: Susan?

BENTLEY: Yeah. She went off like a rocket.

RICHARD: You must have the wrong one. Susan was a lovely girl. She never dropped her tweeds for anyone, not even Simmo. She had the tightest quim in the whole school.

BENTLEY: I've got news for you, mate.

RICHARD: What?

BENTLEY: Simmo had her that night at the last school dance. They had a pump in the bike shed.

RICHARD: How do you know?

BENTLEY: How do I know? I walked in on them, mate.

RICHARD: And Simmo was . . .

BENTLEY: *(nodding)* Chock-a-block.

(Pause.)

RICHARD: *(lamely)* Bulls. Susan wouldn't do a thing like that. She was a lovely girl. Hammo didn't deserve a sister like her.

BENTLEY: Hammo? Sister?

RICHARD: Yes.

BENTLEY: She wasn't Hammo's sister.

RICHARD. Of course she was.

BENTLEY: Hammo's sister was called Doreen.

RICHARD: No it wasn't, it was Susan.

BENTLEY: Doreen.

RICHARD: Susan.

BENTLEY: Fair hair, long legs, and a bum steer?

RICHARD: Black. Black hair. Long black hair.

(Silence.)

Uh, like another grog?

BENTLEY: No thanks.

(Pause.)

RICHARD: Bit on the hot side today. Well, not too hot. Bit warmish, though. It's warmed up a lot.

(Pause.)

BENTLEY: It was quite cool the other morning. I was woken by a breeze very early. A southerly change. I got up and went out for a walk. There's a park near where I live with a pond in it. A few willows, the odd lily, that sort of thing. I used to swing on the willows years ago. It was great fun. Held on tight, got a shove, off I went. Up, up, and away, you know? Then I'd slow down to a dangle. I used to dangle over the pond and then climb up the tree. But when I tried to do it the other morning I fell in. Bloody thing snapped and down I went. Slimy. I got out all wet and then went home to bed. I went back to sleep.

(Pause.)

Yes, it was quite cool the other morning.

(Pause.)

RICHARD: Well, I must be off.

BENTLEY: Righto.

RICHARD: She's all yours.

BENTLEY: Thanks.

RICHARD: I'll leave a note for Gary downstairs and tell him you're the new tenant. You'll like it here. Gary's a good bloke and his Mum cooks a crash hot rissole. Gary's gone away for the weekend, cavorting in the mulga with the Werris Creek Push. You must get him to tell you all about it when he returns. He's a delightful raconteur, in great demand as an after-dinner speaker. You'll like it here. The tap drips in the bog, but otherwise you'll have no worries.

BENTLEY: That's great. I haven't got anywhere to go, you see.

RICHARD: Sure you'll be all right?

BENTLEY: Yes, I'll be all right. I'm going to see if I can find Hammo.

RICHARD: Hammo?

BENTLEY: Yes. Have you seen him? I overheard some blokes talking in the pub about Hammo. Apparently he's running some kind of business. I need a job, you see. Somewhere I can't be . . . got at . . . by anyone. I've got to find Hammo.

(Pause.)

RICHARD: I remember one time some years ago when Gary persuaded me to accompany him on one of his perennial forays into the country. We arrived at this little hick town around dusk. I forget the name of it – someone's gully or creek. I nipped into the pub for a quickie before dinner and I saw Hammo sitting in the corner wearing an old brown overcoat. He was huddled over a brandy by the fireplace. When he saw me, he jumped up with a wild look in his eye and raced out of the back door and on into the foothills. Kept on running till he reached the mountains. His overcoat was billowing out behind him like a parachute, as I remember. I stood on the back step and watched him recede into the distance. It stuck in my mind, that. I never forgot it.

(Pause.)

Well, I must be off.

BENTLEY: Righto.

RICHARD: See you later.

BENTLEY: Don't hit the hops too hard.

RICHARD: Righto.

(RICHARD *opens the door.)*
BENTLEY: Ay Richard.
RICHARD: Yes?
BENTLEY: You're my mate, aren't you? I mean, you
  and Gary, you're my old mates.
RICHARD: Of course.
BENTLEY: You and Gary, you're good mates of mine,
  aren't you?
RICHARD: Of course, we're good mates.
BENTLEY: That's . . . great.
(Pause.)
RICHARD: Goodbye, Ben.
BENTLEY: Goodbye, Dick.
(RICHARD *exits.* BENTLEY *goes up to the pie and looks
at it. He pushes it. It swings to and fro. He watches it.)*

FADE OUT

SCENE TWO

Saturday morning, two weeks later. Lights up on BENTLEY *in bed asleep. He stirs,
wakes up, stretches, and gets out of bed. He plugs in an electric jug and leaves it to boil.
He looks around, goes to the record-player, lifts the lid, pulls out a cup and puts it on
the table. He looks around, then winces and rubs his back. His eyes light up and he
goes to the bed and pulls out a jar of coffee from under the mattress. He puts the coffee
on the table and then looks around again. He turns around, scratching his head, and
bumps into 'Cash and Carry', which rings. The cash drawer pops out and* BENTLEY
*jumps. He looks in the cash drawer and, smiling, pulls out a spoon, which he puts on
the table. He looks around, then goes to the bookcase and runs his finger along the
books. He pulls out a hunk of bread from the bookcase, puts it on the table, then goes
to the back wall and takes down the curved Japanese sword. He cuts a slice of bread
with the sword and nibbles it, grimacing. He puts the sword back and gets the jug,
which is boiling. He brings the jug over to the table, spoons some coffee into the cup
and pours the water in. He looks around, then sneaks over to the door on tip-toe. He
opens the door quietly and peers out cautiously. He sneaks out through the door and
re-emerges a few seconds later, carrying a bottle of milk. He pours a generous quantity
of milk into his cup of coffee, then holds the bottle up. The level of milk is about an
inch from the top. He looks around, picks up the jug, pours some water into the milk
bottle, and then holds the bottle up. It is full to the top. He scampers across the room
like a villain in a silent film and goes out the door. He emerges a few seconds later,
without the bottle, closes the door and goes to the table. He picks up his cup of coffee,*

sips it and goes across to the window. He pulls the curtains back and bright sunlight fills the room. He winces and shields his eyes. He draws the curtains hastily, with an air of decision, puts down his cup and gets back into bed, pulling the blankets over his head.

FADE OUT

SCENE THREE

Saturday night, two weeks later. Lights up on the empty room. It is lit by a blue light over the bed, which casts a dim blue glow over the room. The sound of rain falling gently on a roof is heard. Slow jazz music can also be heard. The room looks a bit tidier and the pie has gone. After a little while, the door opens and GARY comes bursting in.

GARY: Hey poonce features! Are you there?
(BENTLEY *comes in through the passageway. He is half-dressed. During the scene he puts on a clean white shirt, tie etc., and combs his hair.*)
BENTLEY: Hello Gary.
GARY: Phew! What a stink! Smells like King Kong farted.
BENTLEY: I sprayed a bit of the old Airozone around.
GARY: What's all this? Oh I get it, you're setting up for a naughty tonight, are you? Crafty bastard!
BENTLEY: Well, actually, I am thinking of lowering the boom on a young lady I'm taking out tonight.
GARY: You old ram. And to think that all this is going on up here! This used to be a rumpus room for me cousins Craig and Roxanne when they were kiddies. But you'll be up to a different kind of rumpus, won't you? Eh? Bit of a dark horse, aren't you Bentley. Haw! Haw!
(GARY *follows* BENTLEY *all around the room, nudging him.*)
BENTLEY: Ar cut it out, Gary.
GARY: Gunna score between the posts, are you? Haw! Haw!
BENTLEY: Ar jees, Gary.

GARY: Got some frogs under the bed, have you? Haw! Haw!

(BENTLEY *turns on the top light.*)

BENTLEY: All right, Gary, go easy.

(BENTLEY *goes over to a transistor radio on the table and turns off the slow jazz. Then he goes to the record-player and takes off a record. The sound of rain stops.*)

GARY: Righto, mate, don't have a wetty. Just having a friendly go at you.

BENTLEY: I'm aware of that.

GARY: Anyway, what I really mean is, I'm very pleased for you, Bentley. It's about time you had a naughty. This'll be the first you've had since you've been here.

BENTLEY: Oh? What makes you say that?

GARY: Ar come on Bentley, come off it. It's written all over your face. You've been moping round the place like a constipated ostrich ever since you moved in.

BENTLEY: Well, I've been finding my bearings. You've got to have a point of reference, you know. I'm making a comeback.

GARY: And another thing, too. You haven't been outside the front door since you moved in, and it's been four weeks now.

BENTLEY: Well, I haven't sort of got around to going out yet. I'm waiting to hear from Hammo.

GARY: You ought to get out and about more. Look at me and Simmo. We had a great time last night. Went up the country and made a killing on the provincial dogs. Picked up a good tip from a local turf identity. Just as well, though, I lost my shirt on the interstate trots the week before. Went down the mine. We have a great time, me and Simmo. And the tarts! Christ, it's rife up there in the country, mate. Crumpet for the taking.

BENTLEY: Oh? I would have thought that the un-favourable male-female ratio in the rural areas would have mitigated against it.

GARY: That's right, there's lots of crumpet around. Mind you, Bentley, this is just between you and me as men of the world. You wouldn't let on to me Mum, now would you?

BENTLEY: Your secret's safe with me, Gary.

GARY: Thanks, Bentley, you're a real mate. I'm already on the outer with Mum as it is. She put a plate of rissoles down in front of me the other night and I chundered all over them. Too much of the old Resch's. She hasn't said a word to me since, but I'll get around her. Women are all alike, Bentley, you've got to take them with a grain of salt. There's nothing to be afraid of.

BENTLEY: That's for sure. You've just got to know how to handle them, that's all.

GARY: That's the spirit. Get out there and get amongst it. Have one for me, while you're at it.

(He slaps BENTLEY *on the back.)*

BENTLEY: I'll do that, Gary.

GARY: Just assert yourself a bit. Throw your weight around. Remember, in this life it's up for grabs. You've got to go out and get it.

BENTLEY: I'd like to go out and get it, but I don't know where it is.

GARY: Well, anyway, don't let anything stand in your way. Just keep on your toes and walk tall. What you've got to do is stay level-headed and keep your ear to the ground.

(Pause. BENTLEY *thinks.)*

BENTLEY: But that's impossible.

GARY: What is?

BENTLEY: How can you keep a level head when your ear's on the ground? It's impossible. You'd be tilted.

GARY: Tilted?

BENTLEY: Tilted. If your ear's on the ground, your head would be tilted. It wouldn't be level.

(BENTLEY *demonstrates. Pause.)*

GARY: I, uh, see what you mean.

BENTLEY: It'd be impossible to remain level-headed.

GARY: That's a point. That's a very valid point.

BENTLEY: You see what I'm driving at?

GARY: Yes, of course.

(Pause. GARY looks at BENTLEY.)

> Well, I'll be off now, Bentley. Have a good time.
> Hope you don't pick up a dose or put her up the duff
> or anything like that. Who is she, by the way?

*(BENTLEY is now fully dressed, with his hair combed. He
looks in the mirror, then turns to GARY.)*

BENTLEY: Guess.

GARY: Come on, tell me.

BENTLEY: Diane.

GARY: Diane? DIANE?

BENTLEY: That's right.

(GARY laughs.)

GARY: Ar Bentley, you bloody mullet!

BENTLEY: Mullet? What do you mean, mullet?
Everyone calls me that. I'm no mullet, mate, don't
you worry. I'm riding high. I'm on with Diane. It's
all arranged. I'm taking her out tonight and we're
going places. I rang her up and put the hard word on
her. Turns out she's always had a yen for me. Boy,
will Davo be jealous! Huh! He's had his eye on her
for some time, you know, but I'm the pea, she said.
Huh! Will I be on clover! Boy! Old Bentley's done it
again. I'll be –

GARY: So you're a big mover with Diane, are you?

BENTLEY: Practically home and hosed.

GARY: That's interesting.

BENTLEY: Eh?

GARY: I saw Diane tonight. She was getting into
Simmo's B.

BENTLEY: Bulls.

GARY: Simmo's taking her down to the surf club
tonight. She's going to bung on a queue for the life-
savers.

BENTLEY: *(lamely)* Bulls. Diane's a lovely girl. She
wouldn't do a thing like that.

GARY: Simmo's taken her under his wing. He's going to be her promoter. *(Laughing)* If you ask him nicely, he might let you stir the porridge. I mean, after all, you used to bat number ten in the second eleven. You can't expect to go in first drop.

BENTLEY: *(almost inaudibly)* But Diane's a lovely girl.

GARY: That's what the football team reckon. Big mover with Diane! You mullet!

(GARY *goes out laughing.* BENTLEY *sits down on his bed.)*

FADE OUT

SCENE FOUR

GARY *is alone on stage. He is putting up a large banner across the back wall. The banner reads, HAPPY BIRTHDAY, SIMMO. BENTLEY enters through the passageway, carrying a towel over his shoulder. He is whistling. It is a Saturday night, two weeks later.*

BENTLEY: That tap still drips in the bog.

(He sees the banner.)

What's this?

GARY: We're holding a birthday party for Simmo here tonight.

BENTLEY: Here?

GARY: Everywhere. We'll be using the whole house.

BENTLEY: But this is my room.

GARY: We'll need the whole house. It's going to be a real rort. Everyone's coming. All the Manly surf club and a lot of other beach identities. It'll be the turn of the century.

BENTLEY: But look here, you can't –

(RICHARD *and* SANDY *enter. They are both well-dressed, well groomed and prosperous looking.* BENTLEY *stares at them.)*

RICHARD: Hello Bentley.

BENTLEY: Hello Richard.

(Pause.)

GARY: Well, looks like you're the first arrivals.

RICHARD: We're always punctual. Would you like a drink, darling?

SANDY: No thanks. I'll wait till the others arrive.

RICHARD: All right. When's the guest of honour due?

GARY: Pretty soon. Did you bring presents for him?

SANDY: Yes, we left them downstairs with the beach identities.

(SANDY *sits down.*)

GARY: Many there?

RICHARD: Filling up. Davo's there, with Susan and Doreen and the others. Alan White's just arrived. And how are you getting on, Bentley?

BENTLEY: Not too bad. I've been adopting a meaning-ful stance.

RICHARD: That's the shot. Good show.

BENTLEY: How are you getting on?

RICHARD: Very well, thank you. I'm on the board of directors of Simmo Enterprises Ltd.

BENTLEY: You?

RICHARD: That's right.

BENTLEY: That's a bit of a turn-up for the books.

RICHARD: Oh, I don't know. I decided I wanted to be where the action is. There's no percentage in anything else. What's the point of slogging away on the outer? You've got to get on the inside.

BENTLEY: I can't believe it.

RICHARD: Can't you? Simmo decided he'd need my talents.

BENTLEY: What sort of a firm is it?

RICHARD: Well, it's . . . hard to describe. How would you put it, Gary?

GARY: Well, it's difficult to explain, really.

RICHARD: You can't exactly put your finger on it, can you?

GARY: No, not in so many words.

RICHARD: It embraces several concepts, all of which are inter-related to the central core, which in turn is made up of the quintessence of the original concepts, with some allowances for divergences within the framework of the whole.

GARY: That's it in a nutshell.

BENTLEY: Are you a member of the firm?

GARY: Yes.

BENTLEY: What about her?

RICHARD: She's my private secretary. By the way, I've moved into your unit. It's a very nice place.

BENTLEY: What about Simmo?

RICHARD: Oh, Simmo moved out. He's not renowned for monogamy, so I stepped into the breach. We find it a satisfactory arrangement, don't we darling?

SANDY: Very satisfactory.

RICHARD: No hard feelings, old mate?

BENTLEY: I couldn't care less.

RICHARD: Good show. That's the spirit. Well, I see my old room looks much the same. What happened to 'Still Life'?

BENTLEY: I ate it!

RICHARD: You ate it?

BENTLEY: Yes!

RICHARD: Well, quite apart from the metaphysical implications, it must have been a particularly chunderous undertaking. Tell me, what have you been up to?

BENTLEY: Actually, I'm going into business myself.

RICHARD: Really?

BENTLEY: I'm expanding my activities in a number of different directions.

RICHARD: Go on.

BENTLEY: I've established a point of reference. I'm on the up and up.

RICHARD: Glad to hear it.

BENTLEY: Bentley the swinger, that's the good word.

(BENTLEY *moves all over the place, talking excitedly. The others watch impassively.*)

You know, when I married Sandy they all used to whisper behind my back, but I knew what they were saying, I could tell, mate, don't you worry. They were saying, 'How did a poonce like Bentley ever crack on to a horny bird like Sandy?' That's what they said. I heard them, mate, I could tell. But you know what they'll be saying now, they'll be saying, 'How did a swinger like Bentley ever get tied up with a dog-eared tart like Sandy?' That's what they'll be saying, mate, don't you worry.

RICHARD: Why would they say that?

BENTLEY: Why? I'll tell you why. Because Hammo and I are taking over the scene together. That's right. I'm going into business with Hammo. I'm awake up to all the lurks, mate, don't you worry. I've got all the clues. Hammo's got a going concern, he needs a partner for the next stage of development. He said I was the man for the job and that was it. Home and hosed before I knew it. No worries. Boy! I could tell you! Hammo's got a thriving little outfit, don't you worry. Buying and selling, supply and demand. It's simple. Wholesale and retail. It'll be a snack. Hammo said I could be the managing director and he'd see to the rest. Boy! Are we going places! You hear that, we'll be on clover in a couple of years. We'll retire to Coolangatta and buy a penthouse with nude birds running round the terrace and dipping their nipples in our martinis. Me and Hammo, we'll be sitting pretty, I'm telling you. You just watch me and –

RICHARD: Hammo's dead.

BENTLEY: Huh?

GARY: Hammo dropped dead in the pub last night. We got a doctor in, but he was gone.

BENTLEY: Hammo dead?

SANDY: He died of alcoholism. Too much of the 'old Resch's'. It was quite a pathetic case, really. Went on the metho, slept in the park, fell apart at the seams. They took him to a drying-out place, but it was no good.

BENTLEY: Poor old Hammo.

RICHARD: Yes, I felt rather sorry for him. He went quite mad towards the end. Kept on ringing people up and telling them all kinds of weird and wonderful things. He told Davo that Sandy was hot in the pants for him, but Davo subsequently discovered that this was not the case, and copped a black eye for his pains. Yes, I really felt sorry for poor old Hammo. Mind you, he was always a dreamer. Never had both feet on the ground at any given time.

BENTLEY: No business?

GARY: Business? Don't make me laugh. Hammo was on the dole, mate.

BENTLEY: No business.

SANDY: No Hammo.

(Pause.)

BENTLEY: Huh.

RICHARD: Yes.

BENTLEY: Well, huh.

GARY: Yes.

BENTLEY: No . . .

SANDY: Yes.

(Pause.)

BENTLEY: Poor old Hammo. He was a good mate in the old days. Always liked a drink. Remember the time . . . never mind.

GARY: Poor old Hammo. He was a bit funny in the head ever since that time . . . you know . . . at school . . . when Simmo got him in the playground. I saw him once, down by the beach, on the headland there. He was paddling in a rock pool with his overcoat on, and his strides rolled up round his knees. I waved to him, but he didn't see me. He was flying a kite while he paddled. Poor old Hammo.

(DIANE enters briskly. She wears an expensive-looking cocktail dress.)

DIANE: Simmo's arrived. He's downstairs, opening his presents and chatting to the beach identities. He'll be up in a minute.

(Pause.)

What's he doing here?
(They all look at BENTLEY. RICHARD *and* GARY *go over to him.)*

GARY: Uh, look, Bentley, old mate . . . uh . . .

RICHARD: You see, Bentley . . . it's . . .

GARY: Look, Bentley, old mate, we've been good mates for years, and I've always tried to do the right thing by my mates.

RICHARD: So have I.

GARY: But you see, Bentley, there comes a time when . . .

RICHARD: *(gently)* I think he wants you to go, Bentley.

GARY: I'm sorry, mate, but I've got to get with the strength.

RICHARD: You've got to be where the action is.

GARY: It's no good being on the outer.

RICHARD: What's the point of being down and out?

GARY: You've got to get with the strength.

RICHARD: That's lifemanship.

GARY: That's life.

DIANE: Hurry up. Simmo'll be here in a minute.
(Pause.)
   Look, as Simmo's number one girl I insist you get him out of here.

*(*GARY *pulls out a suitcase from under the bed.)*

GARY: I took the liberty of packing your bag while you were in the bath. Mum made you some rissole and pineapple sandwiches. They're in the bag. Unfortunately, Mum omitted the condiments, but I put some tomato sauce in a thermos for you.

RICHARD: Don't judge us too harshly, Bentley.

GARY: I don't like doing this, Bentley, believe me. We've always been good mates. I'm a bloke who always does the right thing by a bloke.

RICHARD: Please don't think too badly of us.

DIANE: For Christ's sake, hurry up.

*(*SANDY *stands.)*

SANDY: Don't make a fuss, Benny. You'll only get hurt. I don't want to see you get hurt.

GARY: You'll have to go out the back way, so you don't bump into Simmo. Goodbye old mate. Have a safe journey.

RICHARD: Goodbye, Bentley.

(BENTLEY *moves slowly across to the passageway, carrying his bag. He stops at the passageway and looks around at them. Silence.*

SANDY *moves a few paces towards him.*)

SANDY: We're very sorry, Benny.

(BENTLEY *looks at her. Pause.* BENTLEY *goes out. Silence.* DIANE *looks through the doorway.*)

DIANE: Here's Simmo now.

(*They all gather round the doorway and start singing, 'Happy Birthday, Simmo'.*)

CURTAIN

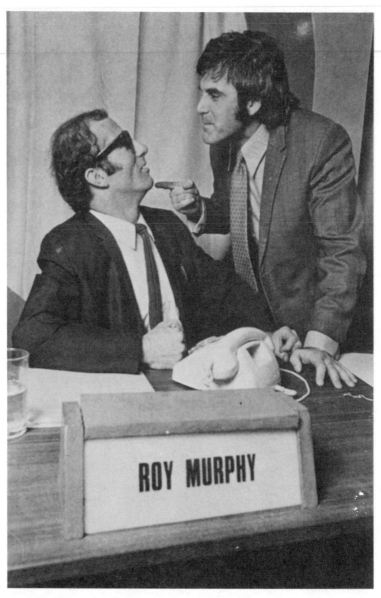

Martin Harris as Clarrie and John Clayton as Roy Murphy in the Nimrod Street Theatre production of *The Roy Murphy Show*, Sydney 1971, directed by Richard Wherrett. Photo: Robert Walker.

The Roy Murphy Show

CHARACTERS

ROY MURPHY, *35, compere of a television sports show*

CLARRIE MALONEY, *55, veteran sports commentator*

MIKE CONOLLY, *25, journalist and sports writer*

SAMUEL T. BOW, *40, coloured Welsh-Jamaican coach of the Manly Rugby League team*

BRIAN CHICKA ARMSTRONG, *20, rugged young Rugby League player*

SHARON, *20, a 'League Maid'*

CHARLES DUNHILL, *30, English, President of the N.S.W. Rugby Union*

COL, *the floor manager*

SCENE

A television studio. Centre stage there is a large semi-circular desk with five name-plates and five seats. The plates read, from left to right, SAMUEL T. BOW, CLARRIE MALONEY, ROY MURPHY, MIKE CONOLLY and CHICKA ARMSTRONG. Behind each name-plate there is a globe, which lights up when the person behind it is on camera. Hung behind the desk is a huge target bearing a large elephant's eye in the centre and scoring rings marked 7, 5, 3 and 1.

NOTE

COL is the floor manager of the TV studio and the stage manager for the play. The parts of SAM and CHARLES are intended to be played by the same actor. When all the desk lights are out, it denotes a pre-recorded commercial break.

The Roy Murphy Show was first performed at the Nimrod Street Theatre, Sydney, on 1st July 1971, with the following cast:

ROY MURPHY	John Clayton
CLARRIE MALONEY	Martin Harris
MIKE CONOLLY	John Wood
SAMUEL T. BOW	Andrew McLennan
SHARON	Jacki Weaver
BRIAN (CHICKA) ARMSTRONG	Marcus Cooney
CHARLES DUNHILL	Andrew McLennan
COL	Larry Eastwood

Setting designed by Larry Eastwood

Directed by Richard Wherrett

Saturday morning, 10 a.m. Lights up on COL *alone on stage, pouring glasses of water at the desk.* ROY *enters.*

ROY: Morning, Col. Getting any? That's the stuff.
(ROY *sits at his place.*)
How about a dry run, Col? Get rid of the gremlins.
(COL *turns* ROY's *light on.*)
Hello there, good morning, God bless and welcome one and all to the World of Sportsview Roundup Highlights on this glorious morning and what a great day it is too! So why don't you sit back, relax, and get with the action for the next sixty minutes. We've got a great show lined up for you this morning, with news, interviews, awards, personalities and stars from the wide and wonderful world of Rugby League. I'll be back in a moment with the top stories of the week. With the top stories of the week. With Col's prick in a plastic bag.
(COL *turns off* ROY's *light.*)
Wake up, Col, the dogs are pissing on your bluey.
(ROY *shuffles some papers on his desk. He sips a glass of water, glances at his watch, then dials a number on the first phone.*)
Diane? Watching the show? Beauty. Hey, I tell you what, can you get away for the weekend? How about The Entrance, her-huh!
(*The second phone rings.*)
Hang on, darls.
(*He picks up the second phone.*)
Hello? Hold the line.
(*He picks up the first phone.*)
Listen darls, I've got to go. Pick you up at twelve, all right?
(*He hangs up and talks into the second phone.*)
Now look dear, you know I wouldn't do a thing like that. A private detective, eh? Photographs of what?

103

(The third phone rings.)
Jesus!
(He snatches up the third phone.)
What the bloody – oh, hello Sir Roland. Yes sir. No
sir. Photographs, eh? Why the bloody –
(His light comes on.)
Hello there, good morning, God bless and welcome
one and all to the World of Sportsview Roundup
Highlights on this glorious morning and what a great
day it is too! So why don't you sit back, relax, and get
with the action for the next sixty minutes. We've got
a great show lined up for you this morning, with news,
interviews, awards, personalities and stars from the
wide and wonderful world of Rugby League. I'll be
back in a moment with the top story of the week.
*(ROY smiles fixedly to the front. His light goes off. He picks
up the third phone.)*
Now look, you know what women are like, Sir Role,
always turning on the waterworks. Sir Roland, I have
never deceived your daughter and the very thought of
indulging in adulterous intrigue is one which I find
repugnant to my sensibilities. Photographs, eh? Of
me and a bird having a –
(ROY's light goes on. He drops the phone.)
Top story of the week was the Sydney Cricket Ground
Trust's refusal to allow Saints and Balmain to play
their Sunday game at the S.C.G. This is just another
example of the Trust's narrow-minded, backward-
looking, pig-headed kind of attitude. If those blokes
up there in their ivory tower would condescend and
have a look around them they'd see that the League
wants Sunday football, the public wants Sunday
football, the clubs want Sunday football, everyone
wants Sunday football except the Trust up in their
corridors of power who are completely, and I stress
completely out of touch with the realities of what goes
on in the world in this present day and age. The
politicians on the S.C.G. Trust sit up there in their
ivory corridors and won't bat an eyebrow at the storm

of protest aroused by their refusal to come to terms with what's going on in the world around them. They're just a bunch of stuck-up old fuddy-duddies and it's about time they got the boot from the blokes in the League who bring in their crust. Who fills the ground? Who makes the turnstiles click? Who earns the Trust a fortune? Rugby League is Sydney's number one spectator sport and the Trust better not bite the hand that feeds them or they'll be out on their ears before much more leather flows over the posts. 'The public be damned' – that's their philosophy and it shows just what a mob of old fogies these blokes are. They're not the sort of blokes who'd have a beer down the pub with a bloke of a Friday night – they're a stuck-up mob with their heads in the clouds and I reckon it's about time they copped the order of the boot. The Rugby League public is sick and tired of the pig-in-a-poke attitude of these dog-in-a-manger dead-heads on the board of directors of the S.C.G. Trust.

(ROY *sips a glass of water.*)

Another chapter in the continuing story of the bungles and follies of officialdom was writ large this week and I reckon it's the sort of thing that's far too prevalent in this day and age. Just listen to this letter I got from a fan in the know:

Dear Roy,

I know you're the sort of bloke who'll have a go so I'm gunna tell you what's goin' on. Last Saturday I was at Redfern Oval sitting down the front and trying to watch the Roosters and the Rabbitos, but all I seen was the backs of the Souths officials. They kept walking up and down the touchline and I couldn't see the game, let alone who it was who laid out Johnny Satto, although my mate reckons it was Jim 'Bazooka' Morgan. What should I do?

(signed) Anxious,

Marrickville.

Well mate, the next time any bungling interfering official gets in the way, give him the big pppfffsshhhh!

(ROY *blows a raspberry. His light goes off. He rustles through his papers. The phone rings. As* ROY *talks on the phone,* CLARRIE *and* MIKE *enter and sit down at the desk.*)

Hello? Yes, Sir Roland. Yes, I see. Indubitably, Sir Roland. Yes, I am in full agreement with the sentiments you have expressed, Sir Roland. You may rest assured that I will endeavour to – thank you, Sir Roland.

(ROY *hangs up. His light goes on.*)

Top story of the week was undoubtedly the disgraceful outburst by a Tiger official, who shall rename maneless, against the S.C.G. Trust for refusing to allow the Saints-Balmain game to be played on the Sydney Cricket Ground. They're a good mob of blokes on the S.C.G. Trust and we ought to give them a fair go.

(*The other lights go on.*)

Well, it's time to introduce the panel to you. Clarrie Maloney, veteran Rugby League commentator (CLARRIE *nods, smiles*) and Mike Conolly, journalist and sports writer (MIKE *nods, smiles*). Righto, now it's time for 'Bets and Threats' and to prove we're men of our word, here we go with the Order of the Red Bandanna for one-eyed Clarrie Maloney, who went for Wests last week but they were beaten by Balmain.

(ROY *whips out a bright red bandanna and ties it over* CLARRIE's *eyes.*)

MIKE: I said I'd clip your toe-nails if the Panthers beat the Bears and they took out the money, so here we go, Clarrie.

(MIKE *pulls* CLARRIE's *foot up on to the desk and whips off his shoe and sock. He starts clipping* CLARRIE's *toe-nails with hedge-clippers.* ROY *brings out a packet of salt and tips some on* CLARRIE's *head, rubbing it in.*)

ROY: And I said I'd rub salt into you, Clarrie, if Eric 'Dim' Simms kicked more than five goals, so here we go with a bit of the old Cerebos.

CLARRIE: (*removing bandanna and removing his foot*) That's enough. Bloody 'Bets and Threats'! What a load of childish codswallop!

ROY: Don't be a bad sport, Clarrie. Before we start the panel debate on last week's TV game, I've got an apology to make for certain statements made on last week's programme by one of our regular commentators. The managing director of this station, Sir Roland Dalrymple, has publicly apologised to the League Board of Control for any misconstrual which may have been placed on a statement concerning the integrity of referees appointed by the Board. Over to you, Mike.

MIKE: I apologise.

ROY: It's all very well to knock the men in white, Mike, but you must bear in mind that referees have many difficulties confronting them and they do have a most insidious task to perform.

MIKE: Of course.

ROY: Okay, let's kick off and start the ball rolling and for openers we'll throw a few curlies at Clarrie Maloney, who predicted a clear-cut victory for the Saints last week. What did you see as the main factors in Parramatta's win, Clarrie?

CLARRIE: Well Roy, it seemed to me that the Parramatta forwards paved the way for the walkover that followed by getting on top of the Dragon pigs in the first twenty minutes. _forwards_

ROY: Mike Conolly.

MIKE: I thought an important factor was the great game played by the Eels' pivot Ivor Lingard. He's a roving utility back and very adept at picking the gap and manoeuvring the defence on to the wrong foot to enable him to distribute the ball to his supports.

ROY: Tell me, Clarrie, who were the stars of the game in your book?

(SAM _enters. He looks to_ COL _for confirmation and then sits at the desk. His light is not on._)

CLARRIE: All six of the Parra pigs, Roy. And for the Saints, Graeme Bowen and the diminutive Billy Smith never gave up.

ROY: He's a little beauty, isn't he Clarrie?

CLARRIE: He'd be one of the gamest little halves I've ever seen. You wouldn't get him up to eleven stone if you dragged him out of the harbour with his overcoat on, but he was tackling blokes twice his weight all day long.

MIKE: He ought to. He's getting five hundred dollars for a win and a hessian jock-strap for a loss.

CLARRIE: What do you mean by that?

ROY: When they build the Rugby League Hall of Fame there'll be a separate wing full of memorabilia recounting the mighty feats of the diminutive Billy Smith.

CLARRIE: I was also impressed by Ronnie Lynch's leadership of the Eels. When Saints went in for that early try, he read the Riot Act behind the line in the old 'Bumper' Farrell style.

MIKE: Who's 'Bumper' Farrell?

CLARRIE: One of the all-time greats of the forties.

MIKE: Oh.

ROY: Right, now it's time to introduce a new addition to our regular panel, and here he is, the colourful coach of Manly, Samuel T. Bow.

(SAM's *light goes on.*)

Good morning and welcome to the World of Sportsview Roundup Highlights, Sam.

SAM: Thanks, Roy.

ROY: I'm sure the viewers at home will be eager to hear the opinions of a man who's worked such wonders with the Manly side, whose position on top of the League ladder is a credit to the efforts of this eminent ebony emigrant. How did you do it, Sam?

SAM: Well, the boys have worked pretty hard, Roy, and they deserve their success.

ROY: Come on, Sam, don't be so modest. Those blokes looked like Brown's cows last year, but you've got 'em really hitting their hobbles and blazing up the comeback trail.

SAM: Well, we've got a long way to go yet, Roy.

CLARRIE: What interests me, Sam, is the way you've got the Manly boys going for the full eighty minutes.

Manly've never been able to come from behind in recent years – they give up the ghost when they lose the lead.

SAM: Well Clarrie, I think I've got the boys to realise that under the six-tackle rule anything can happen and a team that's in front can't close up the game when they've got a handy lead.

ROY: The game's not over till the final whistle goes, eh Sam?

SAM: That's for sure, Roy.

MIKE: You've made a few positional changes since you've been with Manly, Sam. What's behind the shifting of 'Cracka' MacDonald to the wing this week?

SAM: Well Mike, I thought I'd bring Stanton into the centres to contain those two extraordinary fellows Max 'Meteor' Brown and Wayne 'Comet' Peckham, who've proved quite a handful so far this year.

ROY: Horses for courses, eh Sam?

SAM: That's for sure, Roy.

CLARRIE: Tell me, Sam, coming from England as you do, how do you find coaching in Australia?

SAM: I like it very much, Clarrie.

CLARRIE: How do you think the standard of Australian football compares to overseas football, Sam?

SAM: Well, Clarrie, the standard over here's much higher than it is in England.

CLARRIE: You reckon?

SAM: Of course. You wouldn't get a club side in England who could hold a candle to Balmain or Manly. I reckon we'd eat the Wigan team and they're the League champions in England this year.

ROY: A champion team'll always beat a team of champions, eh Sam?

SAM: That's for sure, Roy.

CLARRIE: Anyway Sam, I admire your approach to football and it's a pleasure to have you on the panel.

SAM: Thanks, Clarrie.

MIKE: Yeah, Sam, it'll be good to hear some intelligent comment on the show.

ROY: *(glancing at* MIKE) That goes for me too, Sam. We're very proud and privileged to have you honour us with your presence on the panel of the World of Sportsview Roundup Highlights.

SAM: Thanks, Roy.

(All the lights go off except ROY's.)

ROY: Righto, now before we pause for an important informative interlude, I'd like to reply publicly to a certain columnist who writes for one of the afternoon rags. This ex-cricketer who doesn't know a goal-post from Norm Provan's knee-guard had the temerity, yes, the temerity, to refer to me as Woy, and said I was the biggest watbag on TV and that I knew as much about Rugby League as his Aunt Sally's rheumatic budgerigar. Quite apart from invoking the pot and kettle syndrome, yes, syndrome, this piddling, puerile, pusillanimous, pen-pushing, pie-eating Pariah, yes, piddling, has stooped to the lowest depths of denigration and besmirching by taking umbrage and dudgeon at a certain alleged speech defect of mine which has long since disappeared. To pick on a bloke for a thing like that, well, I tell you what, Sid, you could crawl under a snake in a top hat and stilts. And just for the record, you bugbear, yes, bugbear, my speech impediment has been completely ewadicated ... without a twace ... pppfffsshhhh!

(ROY *blows a raspberry.* COL *hastily switches off his light and all four characters immediately put their feet up, bring out bottles of beer and glasses, sandwiches, cigars, play cards, go to sleep, walk around etc. This goes on for one minute. Then* COL *gives them a signal and there is five seconds of deft, unhurried movement as they conceal everything and face the cameras with fixed smiles. All four lights go on.)*

Righto, I guess it's time to introduce the Footballer of the Week. (BRIAN 'CHICKA' ARMSTRONG *enters.)* It was a (CHICKA *exits)* particularly difficult choice this week as there were so many stars in last week's Balmain-Wests clash, but we selected the best and I'm sure you'll all agree with our choice.

(CHICKA *enters.*) This player's only a young feller (CHICKA *exits*) and he's got a really bright future in front of him. I'll introduce him now, (CHICKA *enters*) but first I'd like to explain (CHICKA *exits*) that we don't give best-and-fairest awards the way Clarrie here does on his radio programme. Rugby League's a man's game, it's a physical contact sport and we don't hold a bit of biff against a player who turns in a blinder. We simply pick the best on the field, and here he is, the rugged young prop from Balmain, the ex-country rep in the City Firsts, the Footballer of the Week, Brian 'Chicka' Armstrong!

(Pause.)

Brian 'Chicka' Armstrong!

(CHICKA *stumbles on as if pushed from behind.* ROY *shakes hands with him.* CHICKA *wears football gear and gym shoes.*)

Welcome to the show, Chicka.

CHICKA: Thanks, Roy.

ROY: That was a great game you played against Wests, Chicka.

CHICKA: Thanks, Roy.

ROY: You turned in a great display of tackling, Chicka, and managed to blot out Wests' fiery red-headed second-rower Barry Bryant. Was this part of a pre-conceived plan?

CHICKA: Yes, Roy.

CLARRIE: I thought veteran Dave Bolton's field goal was the turning point of the game, Chicka. Did you feel you had it won when you hit the front nine-eight with ten minutes to go?

CHICKA: Yes, Clarrie.

MIKE: I noticed right at the start that Balmain kept booting it high to Tony Ford and then following on fast, but after about fifteen minutes you took on the Wests pack and turned the game into a forward battle. Was this because you thought the Wests backs were the main danger, or because you felt the Tigers had the edge in the forwards?

CHICKA: Yes, Mike.

CLARRIE: You're a country lad, Chicka, and it's been quite remarkable the way you've adapted to club football since you've come down to Sydney from Wyong.

CHICKA: Woy Woy.

ROY: Yes yes?

CLARRIE: Do you find you need to be a lot fitter now that you're with Balmain, Chicka, than you did when you were at Woy Woy, or is it more a matter of technique and experience?

(Pause. CHICKA looks at CLARRIE, perplexed. Then his eyes light up, he grins, laughs, and punches MIKE playfully on the arm. MIKE rubs his arm, perplexed.)

ROY: By the, uh, way, Chicka, during last week's game I, uh, noticed you demonstrating your pugilistic prowess in an altercation of fisticuffs with 'Nipper' Maxwell.

CHICKA: Yeah, I jobbed him.

ROY: Ah yes, well, okay Chicka, now it's time for the Commonwealth Bank Passing Competition and you know the rules. Three passes at the target and twenty points to qualify for the finals with big cash prizes and a brand new superseded Toyota sedan to go off. You get ten points for an Elephant's Eye and the Elephant's the symbol of the Commonwealth Bank and it's a pretty good idea to get with the strength. First pass.

(ROY throws CHICKA a football and CHICKA passes it at the target. It goes through the Elephant's Eye and the sound of an elephant's trumpet is heard.)

Wow! Fair in the hole for openers.

(ROY throws CHICKA another football and he does it again.)

Wow! Chicka Armstrong going for the hat trick here.

(ROY throws CHICKA the third ball. Just as CHICKA is about to pass it, SHARON pokes her head through the Elephant's Eye to watch. CHICKA, smitten, passes the ball carelessly and it hits CLARRIE on the head. SHARON disappears.)

Bad luck, Chicka, but chin up, mate, you qualified for the finals with two out of three, and that's no mean feat. In any case, in your capacity as Footballer of the Week, you've won yourself some handsome prizes and to present them to you we've added a touch of glamour to the show and it's a brand new idea thought up by the Rugby League to counteract the Tote-Maids employed by Royal Randwick Racecourse to add a bit of spice to the sport of kings, and so now we've got League-Maids who'll be in attendance at all matches to act as usherettes, hostesses, Girl Fridays, whatever you want to call it without being too rude or making any suggestive insinuendos about the girls' alternate title of Comfort Stations Amenities Attendant. We've got our own resident League-Maid on the World of Sportsview Roundup Highlights, and here she is, the very lovely Sharon!

(SHARON *enters, wheeling a traymobile laden with prizes and brightly coloured packets. She wears a short white skirt, tight red top, and white boots. She has a green and gold sash over her shoulder which reads LEAGUE MAID.*)

SHARON: Hello Boys.

ALL: Hello Sharon.

ROY: Welcome to the Sport of Worldview Roundlight High-Ups, Sharon.

SHARON: Thanks Roy.

ROY: Just get a load of that outfit, fellers, you'll be seeing glamour like this at every game this season. Show the viewers, Sharon.

(SHARON *goes to the front and poses glamorously.*)

Bring it in for a close-up, Col.

(SHARON *continues posing.* ROY *goes around to her, carrying a ruler. He measures the distance between her knee and the hem of her skirt.*)

Ten inches, fellers, how about that? Jees, I tell you what, fellers, it's gunna be difficult to follow the game, eh? Her-huh!

(He puts his arm around SHARON.*)*

Tell us, Sharon, how do you feel about being a League-Maid?

SHARON: It's wonderful, Roy. I'm really wrapped in it.

ROY: Well I must say, Sharon, you've added a touch of glamour to the greatest game of all.

SHARON: Thank you, Roy. All the sports seem to be getting with it these days – football, races . . .

ROY: And the twots.

SHARON: Yes, Roy.

ROY: But, uh, don't get the wrong idea, fellers, these girls aren't just pretty faces. They're been picked for the job because they're also very keen and knowledgeable about the great game of Rugby League.

SHARON: That's very true, Roy, I've been a keen League supporter ever since Richie Benaud played goal-keeper for Maroubra.

CLARRIE: So have I.

ROY: It's great to have you with us as a regular on the show, Sharon, and I must say you League-Maids are more than welcome in the world of Rugby League. It's gunna be hard to keep your eye on the ball, isn't it, Chicka?

CHICKA: Yeah.

ROY: Well Sharon, I guess it's time to present these lovely gifts which have been donated by representatives of the many and varied fields of industrial endeavour to be awarded to our Footballer of the Week, Brian 'Chicka' Armstrong.

SHARON: It'll be a pleasure, Roy. I'm a great admirer of Chicka's and I think he's the sweetest guy playing first grade football.

CHICKA: Ar jees.

ROY: You hear that, Chicka? She's got her eyes on you, boy.

SHARON: Oh, Roy, stop it.

ROY: Well Sharon, what prizes have you got in store for our Chicka, eh? That's not what I meant, Col. Her-huh! He's a lucky man, isn't he Sam?

SAM: That's for sure, Roy.

SHARON: Well Roy, first of all there's the beautiful new Shotgun Gift Pack, comprising a whole range of men's cosmetics.

CLARRIE: Aaah, garn!

(SHARON *picks up a brightly coloured packet from the tray-mobile.*)

SHARON: We've got the Shotgun After-Shave Lotion, Body Talc, Pre-Shave Preparation, Facial Toner, Creme de Cheveux, Shampoo, Anti-Perspirant Deodorant, and a special masculine perfume called Left Hook, which really knocks out the ladies, Chicka. This will do wonders for your charms and sex appeal.

ROY: You'll be fighting them off with a Chick, Sticka.

CHICKA: Yeah?

SHARON: He certainly will, Roy. And I know that Chicka doesn't think there's anything sissy about cosmetics for men, do you Chicka?

ROY: Times are changing, aren't they, Sam?

SAM: That's for sure, Roy.

CLARRIE: Bloody oath they are.

SHARON: That's very true, Roy. The peacock male is here to stay.

ROY: I'm in full agreement with you, Sharon. I heard a bloke say in an airport interview on TV that men are becoming much more fashion-conscious and aware of the latest trends in the cultivation of sex appeal by the judicious application of masculine cosmetics.

SHARON: Yes Roy, auto-eroticism is here to stay and we girls are the ones who benefit.

ROY: What else have you got there for Chicka, Sharon?

SHARON: Well Roy, we've got Mackinlays the Sportsman's Scotch, *(loading* CHICKA *up)* a Taft track suit, Denco-Rub for sore muscles, a Country Club sports shirt, Featherweight Football Boots, a Freddo Frog, a Dunlop Squash Racquet, a Black and Decker Heavy Duty Dual Speed Power Drill, and a very new and useful product, Roy, the Willow Bottle Buddy Iceless Drink Cooler. Isn't it exquisitely elegant?

ROY: By jees yeah, these drink coolers are a really nice looking piece of merchandise and add a touch of class to your dining table. They're used in all the best restaurongs around the town and they look good anywhere, believe you me. I had an ale at City Tatts the other day with Bernie Hamilton, who's the proprietor of one of the highest class restaurongs in town, and he said to me: 'Roy,' he said, 'they'd grace the table of a member of the Royal Family.' And anyone who knows Bernie Hamilton knows he's not misgiven to understatement or over-exaggeration, so I reckon that's a pretty sure bet, the Willow Bottle Buddy Iceless Drink Cooler.

SAM: No sweat, eh Roy?

ROY: That's for sure, Sam.

(SHARON *holds the Cooler for a close-up as* ROY *returns to his place.* SHARON *and* CHICKA *exit.* ROY's *light is the only one on.*)

Right, now it's time for an important announcement. Tomorrow afternoon there'll be a testimonial game for one of the all-time greats of Rugby League, and anyone with an ounce of decency will turn up to Redfern Oval and pay their tribute. Anyone with an ounce, an ounce, one ounce, one ounce of decency, anyone with an *ounce* of decency in their little finger will bend over backwards to lend their support to this testimonial because believe you me and I kid you not ladies and gents one and all, this man had more decency in his little finger than most people have in their little finger, make no mistake about that. This man, *this* man had more than an ounce of decency; he had a ton of guts and always demanded – and got – his pound of flesh. He served with pride in two world wars – put his age up for the first and down for the second and then failed his medicals for Korea and Vietnam. He was one of the greats, one of *the* greats. A contemporary of the legendary Dally Messenger, a confrere of the immortal Dan Frawley, a scholar and a gentleman and a good son to his mother, the world will always remember . . . him . . .

(ROY *has forgotten the man's name and is desperately stalling, feeling around on the desk for a piece of paper. He gestures frantically to* MIKE, *who finally notices him and writes on a piece of paper.*)

... on the beach, in the street, at the pub, down the mine, up the pole, everywhere he was known and revered throughout the land people will always remember *(reading* MIKE's *note)* Roland 'The Pill' Dalrymple. Uh? Mmmh? *(Turning to* MIKE*)* Ppp-fffsshhhh!

(ROY *blows a raspberry. His light goes off. During this commercial break the others read, drink etc.* CHICKA *re-enters wearing a pair of trousers.* ROY's *first phone rings.)*

Yeah? Oh, hello Sir Pim . . . Roland. Yes sir, I'm very sorry. It was a trick, sir, an optical delusion devised by one of my rival enemies. What? But I'm the compere of this show. Look, Sir Roland, I like and respect Mike Conolly as a friend and colleague, but in my humble opinion he's not compere material.

(The second phone rings.)

One moment, Sir Roland.

(ROY *picks up the second phone, glancing at* MIKE.)

Hello? G'day Di. You're in bed, are you darls? Gawww. Wearing my favourite nightie? Gawww.

(The third phone rings.)

Hang on, darls.

(ROY *picks it up. He gets tangled up in the phones.)*

Hello? Oh, hello dear. On what grounds? Photographs, eh? Hold the line.

(He picks up the first phone.)

But look, Sir Roland, think of the publicity. Your rivals in the media will have a field day if your daughter divorces me. The noble name of Dalrymple will become a byword for fraudulent intercourse and illicit malice. Yes. One moment, Sir Roland.

(He picks up the third phone.)

Dear? Now let's not be hasty, eh? Let's talk it over. Good. Hold the line.

(He picks up the first phone, by now completely entangled in cords and receivers.)

I'll be right over after the show, darls. Keep that little pink nightie on, will you? Sir Roland. Uh. Uh. Ah . . . uh . . .

(He hangs up and speaks into the second phone.)

Now look what you made me do, you stupid bitch. Hey, wait on, Di –

(He hangs up and speaks into the third phone.)

Goodbye, dear. What? Look, you great fat camel, I hope your tits drop off so I can flog 'em to the navy as anchors.

(His light goes on. No pause.)

This afternoon we have the first representative match of the season, and here is Clarrie Maloney to give his views on the likely outcome of this encounter.

CLARRIE: About time, too.

ROY: What do you mean by that?

CLARRIE: Well, you've been going on with all the garbage under the sun and haven't said anything about football.

ROY: All right, don't do your block, Clarence Aloysius.

CLARRIE: I will do me block. This is supposed to be a football programme, not a fashion parade.

ROY: Listen to that, will you Sam? Old Clarence Aloysius is going off his little brain.

CLARRIE: It's a darn sight bigger than yours.

ROY: Pppfffsshhhh!

(ROY blows a raspberry.)

MIKE: Anyway, about the City-Country game this afternoon, I reckon it'll be another procession, with City winning by fifty points.

CLARRIE: Don't underrate Country, Mike. They've got a good crop of new blood in their line-up and I reckon they'll really give it a go today.

ROY: I know Sam will agree with me when I say that the battle for possession in the scrums could be an important factor in deciding the issue.

MIKE: It always is, Roy.

(ROY glares at MIKE.)

SAM: On paper, Clarrie, the City side does appear to have the edge, but Brian 'Resch's' Carlson says he's going to have his boys move up fast and bustle the City team right from the start.

MIKE: They'll have the job in front of them trying to stop Billy Smith and Denis Pittard.

CLARRIE: I disagree with you there, Mike, because Pittard can be stopped – look at that grand final when the Tigers tackled him out of the game. Keithy Outten bottled him up like a pickled kipper.

ROY: One of the highlights of the match should be the clash between those two great full-backs, the evergreen Les Johns and –

MIKE: Wayne Williams from Wyong.

ROY: Oh yeah, Rayne Rilliams from Ryong.

CLARRIE: I reckon it's going to be a great game and I forecast that complacency might prove to be City's undoing.

ROY: Clarrie, I would be the last one to deny or deride the tenacious veracity of these boys from the Black Stump and points west, but sheer common logic compels me to tip the City stars to go through 'em like a packet of chalk and cheese.

CLARRIE: What's so great about the City team? A mate of mine, a former representative prop, one of the '59 Kangaroos in fact, reckons that in his humble opinion the lightweight Country pack are more mobile than the overweight, overpaid, so-called City stars.

MIKE: City'll coast home slowing up, Clarrie.

ROY: It'll be a cake-walk.

CLARRIE: It'll be champagne football.

ROY: More like flat beer.

CLARRIE: Neck and neck.

ROY: Ducks and drakes.

CLARRIE: Nip and tuck.

SAM: I think Clarrie's got a point there, Roy, because –

ROY: Look! I don't reckon it's even worth going out to see this game. It's an annual picnic for the City side and I reckon it should be abolished.

CLARRIE: What rubbish! The City-Country game's one of the traditional highlights of the season.

ROY: Get out of it. It's a farce, that game. The City team'll run up more points than you'd find on a porcupine.

CLARRIE: What would you know about it? Those country lads'll dent a few big reputations this afternoon, you mark my words.

ROY: Pig's ar ... pendix! Les Johns'll go through the Country defence like a red-hot poker through a pound of butter.

CLARRIE: You reckon? Les Johns is over the hill, mate. He shouldn't even be in the City Seconds. He's only a shadow of his former self.

ROY: Ar garn! He's head and shoulders above any other full-back playing football.

CLARRIE: Hoh! Bob Smithies'd leave him for dead any day of the week.

ROY: BOB SMITHIES?? He couldn't tackle my crippled grandmother on her way back from the pub.

CLARRIE: Last Saturday, in the match of the day, because of his outstanding defence, I picked Bob Smithies as the best player on the field.

ROY: You couldn't pick your nose.

CLARRIE: I'm a better judge of football than you are, that's for sure.

ROY: You sit there and stick up for the City-Country game and you have the gall to –

CLARRIE: I've got plenty of gall.

ROY: ... the nerve to call yourself a football judge.

CLARRIE: At least I've played the game, unlike certain armchair critics.

ROY: You have not the slightest conception or comprehension of the elementary fundamentals of the noble game of Wugby League.

CLARRIE: I've forgotten more than you ever knew.

ROY: Getting personal, are we Clarrie?

CLARRIE: You're the one who started it by –

ROY: Putting in the verbal boot, are we?

CLARRIE: Look! You reckon you're –

ROY: That's the stuff. Call me names and thump the desk.

CLARRIE: You've got the unmitigated effrontery to –

ROY: Here it comes. Wait for it.

CLARRIE: You bloody well –

ROY: And swearing, too. Would viewers with young children please accept on behalf of –

CLARRIE: *(spluttering)* You ratbag! You're twisting everything I say. You're making me out to be a, well, the very thing you do yourself, you're trying to, you know, turn me into a, you know. It's plain to see what you're about. I'm awake up to you ... you ... twister ...

ROY: *(coolly)* It is obvious to me, quite, quite obvious, in fact it stands out like a black crow in a bucket of milk that you are well past whatever prime you may have once upon a time had.

CLARRIE: And you call yourself a sportsman. What a miscarriage of mockery!

ROY: That's the way. Shoot from the mouth.

CLARRIE: You ought to talk!

ROY: They call Clarrie the 'all night chemist' because he never shuts up and he's always dispensing free purgatives.

CLARRIE: This has been a revelation to me. A real eye-opener.

ROY: I'm glad you admit you're in the wrong.

CLARRIE: I am *not* in the wrong!

ROY: You are so!

CLARRIE: I am not!

ROY: You are so!

CLARRIE: Prove it!

ROY: Prove what?

CLARRIE: Go on!

ROY: Get lost!

CLARRIE: Shut up!

ROY: Make me!

CLARRIE: Oh yeah?

ROY: Yeah!

CLARRIE: Yeah?

ROY: Yeah!

CLARRIE: Yeah?

ROY: Yeah!

(CHICKA *thumps the desk.*)

CHICKA: Hey!

(CHICKA *has been trying to get a word in for some time, raising his finger and opening his mouth. They all look at* CHICKA, *who has forgotten what it was he wanted to say. Pause.*)

Up the Tigers.

(Sighs and mutters all round.)

ROY: Well, as I was saying, I reckon, quite unequivocally and ambivalently, the City-Country game must go.

CLARRIE: I reckon that would be a football tragedy. These country lads work hard all the year and their big incentive is to get picked in the Country team and play on the S.C.G.

ROY: Sentimentality! Pure sentimentality!

CLARRIE: You've got to give the boys from the bush a fair go.

ROY: Slop! Schmaltz! Syrup!

SAM: I think Clarrie does have a point there, Roy.

ROY: No one asked you to butt in with your two cents worth of powdered crap.

SAM: I think Rugby League needs constant revitalising at the grass roots level. If you neglect your regional needs and centralise all your activities in one area, then you get –

ROY: What's he on about, eh? You tell me. What's he on about? I'm at a loss. I don't know what he means. I haven't got a clue. What's he on about, eh? You tell me.

CLARRIE: Let him finish, well.

SAM: I was just trying to make a point, Roy –

ROY: Well I wish you would. I reckon it's about time you made a point. I reckon I'd keel over in a dead faint if you made a point. You've been so bloody devious since you came on this programme I doubt if you could *ever* make a point.

(SAM *stands.*)

SAM: I'm resigning from the programme, Roy. Thanks for having me.

CLARRIE: Now hang on, Sam, don't take any notice of him. Sit down and have your say.

SAM: Thanks Clarrie, but I think I'd better be going. Goodbye.

(SAM *exits.*)

ROY: Well as I was saying about the City-Country game –

CLARRIE: Why did you have to go and do that? What's the matter with you?

ROY: Mind your own business. What do you reckon about the City-Country game, Mike?

MIKE: I think that –

(CHICKA *waves and smiles into the camera.*)

CHICKA: Hullo Mum.

MIKE: I think that Country ought to play Queensland in Brisbane, then in Newcastle, and then combined Country and Queensland should play Sydney in Sydney.

ROY: That's an interesting idea, Mike. In other words, you think the Board of Control's policy is short-sighted and pig-headed in the extreme.

MIKE: Not at all, Roy, but I think traditional policy ought to be modified to suit present needs. With my proposal, you get the best of both worlds.

ROY: Good on you, Mike. It's great to see a young bloke like you speaking out fearlessly against the powers that be and telling the Board of Control to jump in the lake and pull the chain.

MIKE: Hey wait a –

(CLARRIE *thumps the desk.*)

CLARRIE: Now look! You're not being fair to the Country Rugby League, who've given us so many great players over the years.

ROY: Balderdash!

MIKE: Now just a –

ROY: Congratulations, Mike. You're an upcoming young man of sterling integrity. Good on you, son.

(ROY *pats* MIKE, *who flings him off angrily.*)

MIKE: Ar shuddup! You're always trying to drop me in the crap.

ROY: Now, now, Michael, let's not –

(CLARRIE *thumps the desk.*)

CLARRIE: You're being detrimental to the future of the game.

ROY: Baloney!

MIKE: I'd like to –

(CLARRIE *thumps the desk.*)

CLARRIE: I reckon the country lads deserve a break.

(CHICKA *thumps the desk.*)

CHICKA: Up the Tigers!

ROY: Pppfffsshhhh!

(ROY *blows a raspberry.* COL *hastily switches off the lights.* ROY, MIKE, *and* CLARRIE *go purposefully behind the target, where a wild fight ensues. The target takes a battering and sounds of punches and muffled cries are heard spasmodically.* COL *tears his hair. Meanwhile,* SHARON *has entered and leads* CHICKA *over to the front of the stage.*)

SHARON: I've got a very mess – *(catching herself, with a whistle and smile)* special message for all the gentlemen watching the show and it's one which concerns the ladies too. One of the prizes on our Rugby League programme is a pair of Stax Slax from the House of De Saxe, and it's a prize we give to all our award winners before they come on the show. Brian 'Chicka' Armstrong, the leg-spinner from Balmain, is our Footballer of the Week, and he's wearing his Stax Slax. How do they feel, Chicka?

CHICKA: Great.

SHARON: Move around a bit and let the viewers see how they look, Chicka.

(CHICKA *models, poses, walks around. He bumps into the desk.*)

How do they fit, Chicka?

CHICKA: Great.

SHARON: Notice the way they ride snugly on the hips, viewers, and also the tapered thighs and slight flare at the ankle. They're available in all bright hues for the peacock male and checks and stripes as well as the new imported 'Machismo' line in two-tone colours of curry and gold. They're made from corded polyester and pleated dacryl with a glazed woven fibreglass belt and lacquered chrome buckle with acrylic vinyl pocket buttons, and they're ideal for that Saturday party or Sunday barbecue. What's your verdict on the Stax Slax from the House of De Saxe, Chicka?

CHICKA: Great.

SHARON: Well, there you are, boys, if you want to look like Brian 'Chicka' Armstrong, Balmain's champion decathlete, you buy yourself a pair of groovy Stax Slax from the House of De Saxe.

(COL *holds up an idiot board.*)

CHICKA: You can relax in Stax.

(*They smile fixedly.* ROY, CLARRIE, *and* MIKE *emerge from behind the target. They look dishevelled and chastened. They all resume their places at the desk.* SHARON *exits, and the lights come on.*)

ROY: Well viewers, I'll just ask our panel to sum up the big game this afternoon. Mike Conolly.

MIKE: I think City should win, but I think Country could win too. Both sides have many good players and it should prove to be a most interesting and entertaining game with lots of . . . oh hell! City to win by fifty points!

ROY: Clarrie Baloney . . . Maloney.

CLARRIE: I predict that this'll be a close one which could go either way. On paper, City looks the stronger side, but they're only a collection of individuals and I reckon Country's superior teamwork will prove the deciding factor. Country to win by a whisker.

ROY: Chicka Armstrong.

CHICKA: Yes, Roy?

ROY: What's your tip?

CHICKA: I reckon we'll eat 'em.

ROY: Well, my own tip, in my own opinion, is City to win by a country mile. The bushwhackers have been weakened this year by the loss of Don 'Chopper' Pascoe, and although Brian 'Resch's' Carlson reckons he's got an exciting young prospect from the Illawawa awea by the name of . . . what's that kid's name?

MIKE: Rory Raymond.

ROY: That's the one. A youngster from the Ill . . . near Wollongong. Still, all in all, little Audrey heard that as sure as God made little green apples, Country'll go down for the count this afternoon, despite City selection blunders like the shock omission of veteran Ken Irvine and the surprise inclusion of tyro hooker Kel Brown. What a way to wun a wailwoad! Well, there you have it, viewers, the panel votes by three to one, City to win. So put all your money on Country, eh? Her-huh!

(ROY *stands.*)

Righto, now it's time to show you some really exciting products from the Home of Sport, Mick Simmons.

(ROY *goes over to the side of the stage where* COL *has put a weight-lifting set. The desk lights go off.* MIKE *beckons for more beer.*)

This is the new Mick Simmons body-building set, which is guaranteed to make a man out of you in six months or your money back.

(*Meanwhile,* SHARON *comes out with the beer and refills* MIKE's *glass.* MIKE *grabs her and kisses her, and they roll over on top of the desk.* CHICKA *watches enviously.*)

I, uh, haven't started on my course yet, fellas, as you might have guessed – now cut it out, Col. This here's the dumb-bell – righto, Col! Now all you have to do is lift it. Jees, I dunno if I can. (*Grunting and trying to lift the dumb-bell*) I tell you what, fellas, it's the old story of don't do what I do, do what I say. Jees, I can't lift the dashed thing. Ar shut your face, Col.

(Meanwhile, MIKE *and* SHARON *have dived passionately under the desk,* MIKE *more passionately than* SHARON. ROY *struggles with the weights, falls over and gets tangled up in them.)*

Jees, I tell you what, fellas, it's a case of too much hops down the City Tatts. *(Grunting)* They're certainly not made for weaklings, these weights. I bumped into Johnny Raper in the Turkish Bath at Tatts, and he reckons this is the ideal method of keeping fit and up to the mark. Yeah, I know, Col.

(SHARON's *top and sash fly up in the air and land on the floor in front of the desk, followed by her skirt.* ROY *manages to extricate himself from the weights and stands up. He nervously kicks* SHARON's *clothing away as he speaks.)*

Anyway, fellas, there it is, what more can I say? The Mick Simmons Home of Sport Body-Building Set comprising eight hundred pounds of weights, one cross-bar and two dumb-bells, priced at seventy dollars for the lot. Guaranteed to make a man of you in six months or your money back. I'll buy one for you, too, Col. Right, now it's back to the panel.

(He crosses back to the desk. MIKE *and* SHARON *are still underneath.)*

Righto, now I guess it's time to discuss Sunday's round of club games. First of all, there's Norths versus St. George at the Sports Ground. Chicka Armstrong.

CHICKA: Yes, Roy?

ROY: Who do you tip to win, Chicka?

CHICKA: City, Roy.

ROY: Who do you think will win the Norths-St. George match?

CHICKA: A draw.

ROY: Then there's the Canterbury-Manly clash at Brookvale Oval.

(The phone rings.)

Hello? Oh, hello Sir Roland.

(He puts his hand over the receiver.)

Clarrie Maloney.

(ROY *talks quietly into the phone. His light goes off.)*

CLARRIE: I've got to go for Manly to win this one. Sam Bow's got his boys on the crest of a wave and I think they'd down the Berries blindfolded.

(ROY's *light goes on.*)

ROY: Indubitably, Sir Roland. Oh, uh, yeah, then there's Wests versus Easts at Lidcombe Oval. How do you see this one, Mike Conolly?

(ROY *resumes his telephone conversation. His light goes off and* MIKE's *comes on.* MIKE *pops his head up quickly but calmly.*)

MIKE: You've just got to go for Wests this week, despite their defeat by Balmain last Saturday. Wests have got too much weight in their pack and Steve Winter's going to prove a handful for the lighter Easts men.

(ROY's *light goes on.* MIKE *disappears under the desk.*)

ROY: Of course, Sir Roland. Oh, uh, then there's England versus Wales, no, uh, the Green Pay Backers, wait on, oh yes, Balmain and Newtown at Henson Park. Chicka Armstrong.

(CHICKA's *light goes on. He thumps the desk.*)

CHICKA: Up the Tigers!

(Pause. ROY's *light goes on.)*

ROY: Of course I'll be nice to him, Sir Roland. Toujours la politesse. Oh, uh, well, uh, Penrith and Parramatta at Penrith Park. Clarrie Maloney.

CLARRIE: This local derby looks like being the battle for the wooden spoon, with Bobby Boland's boys having a slight edge over Jack Argent's mob, despite the welcome return to form of 'Moby' Dick Thornett. I go for Penrith by a short head from Argent's Pies in a photo finish.

(ROY's *light goes on.*)

ROY: Indubitably, Sir Roland. Oh, uh, where is it? South Sydney versus Cronulla at Endeavour Field. Mike Conolly.

(MIKE's *light goes on.* SHARON, *clad in a bra, bobs her head up, looks astonished, and disappears.* MIKE *bobs up.*)

MIKE: This looks like being the Year of the Rabbit and I reckon they'll trounce the Sharks by a cricket score. Souths have got speed, youth, weight, Johnny Satto, and . . . a . . . lot . . . of . . .

(MIKE *disappears.* ROY's *light goes on.*)

ROY: Yes. Yes. Yes. One moment, Sir Roland.

(SHARON, *clad in bra, panties and white boots, crawls around the corner of the desk. She retrieves her sash, top and skirt.* MIKE *crawls around after her, minus his trousers, as* ROY *talks.*)

Well, there it is, viewers, the panel have tipped Manly, Balmain, Penrith, Souths and Wests to win and *(glancing at* CHICKA*)* Saints and Norths to play a draw. So it looks as if nobody's tipping an upset, although it's hard to tell with so many –

(SHARON *has climbed on the desk to retrieve her clothing. She now realises she is on camera and smiles, aghast. She gurgles and looks horrified, and jumps through the Elephant's Eye. The sound of the Elephant's trumpet is heard.* MIKE *chases her and dives through after her. The trumpet sound is heard again.* CHICKA, *panting, rushes over and dives through after them. The sound of a huge cash register is heard, lights flash, beeping noises fill the air, and a red banner with JACKPOT written on it flops down from above.* ROY *speaks into the phone.*)

I think you could file that under circumstances beyond our control, Sir Roland.

(ROY *holds the phone at arm's length, a pained expression on his face.*)

Well, that just about wraps up our Rugby League segment for today, but I'll be back in just a minute for a brief summary of this afternoon's Rugby Union round. You can't win 'em all, eh Clarrie?

CLARRIE: That's for sure, Roy.

(The lights go off. CLARRIE *exits.)*

ROY: *(into phone)* No, Sir Roland. Never again. Is she? Good. You've got a very sensible daughter, Sir Roland. Well, yes sir, I must agree Mr Conolly has earned himself the bullet by his disgraceful misdemeanour. Good. Thank you, Sir Roland, I'd be happy to continue to serve you in this capacity and I trust your evident mispleasure with me will undergo a rapid transformation. See you on the first tee at nine, Sir Role.

(ROY *hangs up. The second phone rings.*)

Hello? Oh, g'day Di. No, I'll have to give it a miss. Home and hearth won out in the end. It's my job. No, I don't enjoy it, although tell me that when I was a kid and I would've said you were mad. No, I don't enjoy it darls, and I've come to hate sport, but you've got to hang on, haven't you darls? I mean, that's living, isn't it? You've got to hang on. Diane? Hello? You bitch!

(ROY *hangs up.*)

Phew! You must have had kittens during that attempted naughty, eh Col?

(CHARLES DUNHILL *enters.*)

Charles, isn't it? Do sit down.

(CHARLES *sits in* SAM's *place.*)

Had a bit of strife there with Mike Conolly, eh? He was tipped as my likely successor, you know. Sir Roland was momentarily flirting with the idea of dispatching with my talents.

(*Their lights go on.*)

Ladies and gentlemen, we have a most distinguished guest on our Rugby Union segment this morning and it is with great pride and pleasure that I introduce the new chairman of the New South Wales Rugby Union, Mr. Charles Dunhill.

(CHARLES *nods.*)

Well, Charles, you've only been in the country a little while and I'd like to ask to what do you attribute your meteoric ascendancy.

CHARLES: Actually it was quite simple, really. My father, Sir Philip Dunhill, made a few phone calls from London and here I am.

ROY: Fair enough. What sort of football background do you have, Charles?

CHARLES: Oh dear, let me see now. I was third reserve for the fourth fifteen at Eton, and I saw the Welshmen at Twickenham about six years ago.

ROY: What about your more recent activities, Charles?

CHARLES: Well, for the last ten years I've been a somewhat peripatetic student at the Polytechnic Art School in London. That is, until my father decided I should indulge in more rigorous pursuits.

ROY: Good on you, Charles. You bring a wealth of experience and expertise to your position which I'm sure will enrich and invigorate the local Rugby Union scene. You feel you're settling into your new position all right, Chuck?

CHARLES: Oh yes, quite well, thank you. We've run out of scotch a couple of times, but otherwise it's been quite pleasant.

ROY: They're a good mob of blokes down there at the Rugby Union, aren't they Chilla?

CHARLES: They're a scream, an absolute hoot. I've never met such a bunch of droll fellows in all my life. I feel I'm rapidly approaching an understanding of the sort of quintessential contemporary high campery of the Antipodean mentality.

ROY: Yesiree. Anyway Charles, I'd like to extend a warm welcome to you and I hope you'll come down and have a beer with me at City Tatts. It's a very high class place, Charles, and I think you'd appreciate it.

CHARLES: City Tatts? I wouldn't be seen dead in that common little dive.

ROY: Good on you, mate. There's nothing stuck-up about you, Charles. You don't put on airs.

CHARLES: I don't need to.

ROY: Well Charles, now it's time to pause for a commercial word from our sponsor, who makes all this possible.

(*The lights go off.* ROY *comes around the front of the desk.* CHARLES *lights a cigarette and looks languidly around.*)

You know, time was when summer came round you'd need a fan to keep you cool and an iron to keep the creases out of your strides. But not any more, because with Roger Carlyle suits made from the new micro-weave miracle fibre polydaclon, you're kept in cool creaseless comfort all summer long. How do you get a Roger Carlyle suit and why are we advertising them in winter? Well, I'll tell you. If you trade in your old suit now, you get a terrific off-peak twelve-twelve warranty with a double indemnity third party guarantee on your trade-in re-sale. Does that answer your question? Just get a load of these Roger Carlyle suits, eh? *(Modelling)* I'll lay my word on the line and say they're the best that money can buy. So take a tip from me and get yourself down to Roger Carlyle for this once-in-a-lifetime offer, and tell 'em Roy sent you.

(He winks sincerely and grins into the camera, then turns to resume his place at the desk. CHARLES, *however, has moved around and occupied* ROY's *seat as the phone rings.)*

CHARLES: Hello? Oh, hello Roland. What? Roland, I couldn't possibly. I don't know how to compere a sports show. Have I? Do I? Well, thank you, Roland. My father? I see. Oh, all right, I'll start next Saturday. Bye. *(He hangs up)*

ROY: But . . . you can't . . . this is . . . this is . . .

(The lights come on. ROY *sits at* CHICKA's *place.* CHARLES *settles back and looks around his new domain.)* Well Charles, there's a full round of Rugby Union this afternoon and here it is. Gordon versus Drummoyne, Manly versus Sydney Uni – should be a good one, Charles.

CHARLES: Should be a good one, Roy.

ROY: Wests versus New South Wales Uni, Randwick versus Norths – should be a good one, Charles.

CHARLES: Should be a good one, Roy.

ROY: Easts versus St. George, Parramatta versus Eastwood.

CHARLES: Should be a good one, Roy.

ROY: Should be a good one, Charles.

CHARLES: Thank you, Roy. You've been so nice.

(CHARLES *picks up* ROY's *name-plate and throws it away.*)

ROY: *(broken)* Well Charles, all that wemains for me to say is that you're a good bloke and I'm sure you'll get a fair go out here. I feel sure that under your guidance and wisdom the fount of Wugby Union will pour forth gweat glowy and wiches and you will pweside over the dawn of a new ewa in football which will come to be wecorded by the scwibes and pundits for postewity as a golden age of Wugby Union and it will be a twibute to you as a good bloke and as a man of foresight and vision to whom good blokes evewywhere will pwoudly dip their humble lids. Is there anything you'd like to add in conclusion, Charles?

CHARLES: Pppfffsshhhh!

(CHARLES *blows a raspberry.*)

BLACKOUT

Marcus Cooney as Chicka, Martin Harris as Clarrie, Jacki Weaver as Sharon and John Clayton as Roy in the Nimrod production of *The Roy Murphy Show*. Photo: Robert Walker.

Helen Morse as Sandy in the Nimrod production of *Rooted*. Photo: Anthony Horler. Jack Murdock and Barbara Caruso in the Hartford Stage Company production of *Rooted*. Photo: David Robbins.

NOTES AND GLOSSARY

Some of the names in **Rooted** reflect the common Sydney school-boy practice of creating nick-names by adding 'o' to the first syllable of a surname. Thus, for instance, Hammond would become Hammo. First names may be treated in the same way—Jacko, Davo.

While the characters in **The Roy Murphy Show** are entirely fictitious, the rugby league teams they discuss (usually under their familiar nick-names) are real; as are also the star players referred to—Norm Provan, Johnny Raper. Only the 'League-Maid', Sharon, is ill-informed on rugby league: Richie Benaud is, of course, a cricketer, not a footballer; there is no Maroubra rugby league team; and the game requires no goal-keeper. Sydney's major rugby league teams include:—

Canterbury-Bankstown (the Berries); Cronulla-Sutherland (the Sharks); Eastern Suburbs (the Roosters); Manly-Warringah(the Seagulls, the Sea Eagles); Newtown (the Bluebags, the Jets); North Sydney (the Bears); Parramatta (Parra, the Eels); Penrith (the Panthers); Saint George (Saints, the Dragons); South Sydney (the Rabbits, the Rabbitos); Western Suburbs (the Magpies).

AIF, Australian Imperial Force, the voluntary Australian Army.
Alice Springs, the isolated chief town of central Australia. So, *from Alice Springs to breakfast time*, from one end of the country to the other, everywhere.
Anzac, Australian and New Zealand Army Corps. Australia's contingent to World War I.
B (colloquial), an M.G.B., the 'B' model of the M.G. sports car.
Balmain, an industrial harbourside Sydney suburb.
Bears, the North Sydney rugby league team, Norths.
Benaud, Richie, an Australian test cricketer and captain.
Billy-cart, a child's vehicle, often little more than a box on wheels.
Blinder (colloquial), a dazzling display of skill, especially in sport.

Bliss, Johnny, rhyming slang for piss.

Block (colloquial), head; thus *to do your block*, to lose your temper.

Blokes (colloquial), fellows.

Bludger (colloquial), one who avoids work and lives off other people; often used without precise reference as a general term of abuse.

Blue (colloquial), a fight.

Bluey, a swag, the outback tramp's roll containing his blanket and other belongings. *The dogs are pissing on your bluey*, wake up; or, more generally, something unpleasant is happening to your little world.

Bog (colloquial), lavatory.

Boongs (colloquial), a pejorative term for aboriginals, by extension, any black or coloured people.

Botany Bay, a bay just south of Sydney, the scene of Captain James Cook's first landing on Australian soil.

Bronte, a seaside Sydney suburb.

Brown's cows, like, in single file, in a straggling manner.

Buck the system, rebel, in the manner of a bucking horse.

Buckley's, or **Buckley's chance,** no chance at all. Derived from a pun on the name Buckley & Nunn, a well-known Melbourne department store.

Bull (colloquial), abbreviation of bull-dust or bull-shit, nonsense. *To bung on the bull*, to put on airs, to behave pretentiously.

Bung (colloquial), to put. See bull, also side.

Burp, to eructate; thus *burp a rainbow*, to vomit.

Centennial Park, a large Sydney public park to the south-east of the city.

Cerebos, a brand of table salt.

Chop, cut, from the best cut of the carcase. Thus, *to be in for your chop*, to participate in a project for what you can get. *Not much chop*, of little value.

Chops (colloquial), jaws; *flog your chops* (derivation obscure), wear yourself out.

Chows (colloquial), Chinese.

Chuck (colloquial), vomit.

Chug-a-lug, a drinking toast.

Chunder (colloquial), vomit.

Cluey (from clue; also *to be clued up*, *to have the clues*), clever; intelligent, knowing the right information.

Coot (colloquial), a foolish person.

Crap on, go on talking nonsense.

Creamer (colloquial), someone who is over-excited or scared; by implication not in control of his emotions or affairs.

Creek, as in *up the creek without a paddle*, in a desperate or impossible situation.

Crool, or **Cruel,** to damage; thus *to cruel one's pitch*, damage one's own interests.

Cross, The, King's Cross, an inner suburb of Sydney noted for its night-life.

D.A., Resch's Dinner Ale, a Sydney beer.

Dim Sim, a small roll made of paste filled with meat and vegetables, originally a Chinese recipe but now mass-produced in Australia.

Dixon Street, the main street in the Sydney Chinese quarter.

Dragons, Saints, the Saint George rugby league team.

Entrance, The, a holiday resort at the mouth of Tuggerah Lake, north of Sydney.

Fang, to drive a car fast and in an aggressive manner.

Fantales, an old-established brand of chocolate-coated toffees, distinguished by the biographies of film stars printed on the wrapping papers.

Flaggers, in, in flagrante delicto.

Flynn, in like (also **in like Errol**), refers to the athletic and sexual prowess of the late Australian-born Hollywood actor.

Frog (colloquial), from French letter, a prophylactic sheath.

Gallipoli, the site on the Dardanelles where the Australian and New Zealand Army Corps engaged Turkish forces in 1915, during World War I. Though a disastrous failure the campaign was distinguished by the gallantry of the Anzac forces, and returned soldiers from the campaign command a special respect. Anzac Day, April 25th, is Australia's national day of remembrance for those killed in action in World War I and subsequent wars.

Get with the Strength, an advertising slogan of the Commonwealth Bank of Australia, the emblem of which is an elephant.

Grunter (colloquial), a promiscuous girl.

Gyppos (colloquial), Egyptians, Arabs.

Harold Park, a Sydney trotting and greyhound racing track.

Hobbles, hitting their, (of horses) galloping despite hobble-chains.

Holden, Australia's most popular make of car, manufactured in Australia by General Motors Holden.

Hyde Park, a public park in the city of Sydney.

Illawarra, a fertile area around Lake Illawarra, south of Sydney.

Job (colloquial), as in *job him, job him one*, to hit.

Kero (colloquial), kerosene.

Knuckle sandwich (colloquial), a blow to the mouth.

La Perouse, a seaside suburb south of Sydney, near Captain Cook's landing place. It has a fairly large coloured population.

Leagues Club, one of a chain of New South Wales social clubs established by rugby league team supporters, which provide luxurious leisure facilities for their members. The chief income of these clubs, many of which are worth millions of dollars, is derived from the poker machines which New South Wales law permits to be operated in registered clubs.

Leichhardt Oval, a football ground in Sydney.

Lone Pine, one of the ridges of Gallipoli.

Lurk (colloquial), a crafty dodge.

Maroubra, a south-eastern beach suburb of Sydney. There is no Maroubra rugby league team.

Marrickville, a south-western Sydney suburb.

Middy, a ten fluid ounce beer glass.

Miranda, a southern Sydney suburb.

Moral, a, a moral certainty.

Mulga, name given to various species of *Acacia*, especially *Acacia aneura;* colloquially, a general term for ragged bushland.

Neg driving, negligent driving.

Niner, a nine-gallon keg.

Panthers, the Penrith rugby league team.

Parra, Parramatta, the Parramatta rugby league team.

Pervs (colloquial), perverts, often specifically voyeurs; often used as a pejorative term for men who like watching girls.

Pies, Sargent's, a popular Sydney make of the distinctive Australian meat pie manufactured in enormous numbers.

Pigs, Rugby League forwards.

Pisspot (colloquial), drunkard.

Pole, up the (colloquial), in a terminal situation.

Poofter (colloquial), a pejorative term for a male homosexual or any man with artistic or not overtly 'masculine' interests.

Poonce, variant of ponce.

Pros and Cons, prostitutes and convicts.

Put away (colloquial), to gaol.

Quim (colloquial), female genitalia.

RSL, The Returned Services League, an influential organisation concerned with the welfare of returned servicemen and their families but also an active and conservative political lobby.

RSL Club, one of a chain of social clubs established by suburban branches of the RSL, similar to the Leagues Clubs (*q.v.*).

Rabbitos, Rabbits, Souths, South Sydney rugby league team.

Rats of Tobruk, members of the Australian Imperial Force who held off German forces against overwhelming odds at the Battle of Tobruk in 1942. According to the German commander, Rommel, they were trapped in Tobruk like rats. The term became a badge of pride.

Red Ned (colloquial), rough red wine.

Resch's, a popular Sydney brand of beer.

Roosters, Easts, the Eastern Suburbs rugby league team.

Root (colloquial), sexual intercourse; thus *weekend root*, a casual partner. To be *rooted*, to be ruined, trapped, without resource.

Rort (colloquial), from rorty; a riotous gathering or party.

Rubbity, from rubbity-dub, rhyming slang for pub (public house).

Scrap (colloquial), fight, battle.

Screw (colloquial), gaze; from the act of screwing up the eyes against the sun to see at a distance.

Sell the dump to a mate, a rugby league term meaning to pass the ball to a team mate in order to avoid being tackled oneself; generally, to pass the trouble to someone else.

Sharks, the Cronulla-Sutherland rugby league team.

She's right (colloquial), all is well.

Shine (colloquial), liking; used only in the expression *to take a shine to someone*.

Shoot through (colloquial), depart summarily, clear out.

Side, affectation; *to bung on side*, to behave pretentiously or affectedly.

Souths, the South Sydney rugby league team.

Spit, the big, vomit.

Sport (colloquial), one who joins in communal activities, a fair-minded person. Thus *a good sport*, a popular fellow, a good loser; one of the Australian's highest terms of praise.

Strides (colloquial), trousers.

Super (colloquial), superannuation benefits.

Tigers, the Balmain rugby league team.

Tote, totalizator.

Traymobile, a tea-trolley.

Turn (colloquial), a party, a formal gathering.

Unit, home unit, a small apartment.

Walloper (colloquial), policeman.

Werris Creek, a country town in north-western New South Wales.

Wests, the Western Suburbs rugby league team.

Wobbly, from Wobblies, the nick-name for the Industrial Workers of the World. The Wobblies are chiefly remembered in Australia for a sequence of events in Sydney between 1916 and 1920 involving militant and often violent left-wing activities.

Wollongong, coastal industrial city south of Sydney.

Woy Woy, a holiday resort north of Sydney near the mouth of the Hawkesbury River.

Wyong, a town north of Sydney.

Also by Alexander Buzo

Macquarie
This play investigates the predicament of the liberal in a position of authority, counterpointing the situation of Governor Lachlan Macquarie in the early days of the colony of New South Wales with that of a university lecturer in History in the present day.
Introduced by Katharine Brisbane. Preface by Manning Clark.

Coralie Lansdowne Says No
Coralie is about to turn 30 and is faced with three men who want her, each in a different way, and none of them promising to fulfil her ideas for a relationship. Trapped, ambushed, surrounded by cripples of one sort or another, this brilliant character flails about with all her resources before succumbing to a compromise. The book is introduced by Ken Horler, who directed the long-running Nimrod production in 1974.

Martello Towers
Described by Margaret Jones as a sort of 'Pittwater-style French farce', this is a comedy of affluent Australian manners. Edward Martello, unkindly witty and feckless, escapes to an island fortress holiday home, only to be faced by his estranged wife and her disc jockey lover, his devoted sister, his Italian father and his establishment mother-in-law. Introduced by theatre directors John Sumner and Richard Wherrett, with Buzo's comment on the critical controversy the play aroused.

Big River, The Marginal Farm
Australia as a maturing woman devoting her life to the nurture of an unwanted backwater? Or an alienated romantic eking out an arid coexistence with her Pacific neighbours? The ironic questions lie behind Buzo's domestic dramas. In *Big River* we see the rural Hindmarsh family at the moment of Australia's Federation, bury the pioneering spirit and old imperial graces and turn to the cultivation of greater suburbia. *The Marginal Farm*, set against the sugar industry of Fiji in the 50s, is a portrait of corporate colonialism, breeding transients and fringe-dwellers. At the heart of the plays are Adela Learmonth and Toby Parks, high-flying, immature women whose pursuit of happiness is the battle ground for these conflicts. Introduced by John McCallum and Aarne Neeme.